Hebrews
Quick Study Commentary

By Chad Sychtysz

© 2025 Spiritbuilding Publishers.
All rights reserved. No part of this book may be reproduced in any form without the written permission of the publisher.

Published by
Spiritbuilding Publishers
9700 Ferry Road, Waynesville, Ohio 45068

HEBREWS PERSONAL WORKBOOK
By Chad Sychtysz

ISBN: 978-1-964-80537-5

Spiritbuilding
PUBLISHERS

spiritbuilding.com

Table of Contents

Introduction 1
Section One: The Supremacy of Christ (1:1—2:18) 14
Christ Is Heir of All Things (1:1–3) 14
Christ's Supremacy over Angels (1:4—2:4) 19
Christ's Supremacy over Humankind (2:5–18) 24
Section Two: Warnings against Apostasy (3:1—6:20) 33
First Warning against Apostasy (3:1–19) 33
The Danger of Forfeiting What Was Promised (4:1–13) 38
Christ as Our High Priest (4:14—5:10) 44
Second Warning against Apostasy (5:11—6:20) 48
Section Three: A New Priesthood and Covenant (7:1—10:18) 56
The New Priesthood Not Based on Law (7:1–22) 56
Comparison of the Two Priesthoods (7:23—8:13) 62
A New Covenant in Christ's Blood (9:1–22) 73
Christ's Once-for-all Offering (9:23—10:18) 83
**Section Four: The Need for Greater Faith and Endurance
(10:19—12:29)** 91
Third Warning against Apostasy (10:19–39) 91
Faith and Those Who Have Exemplified It (11:1–40) 101
The Need for Focus and Discipline (12:1–17) 115
The Unshakable Kingdom (12:18–29) 124
Section Five: Final Admonitions (13:1–25) 132
Christian Responsibilities (13:1–19) 132
Benediction and Final Thoughts (13:20–25) 143
Sources Used for This Study 146

Scripture taken from the NEW AMERICAN STANDARD BIBLE®,
© 1960, 1962, 1963, 1968, 1971, 1972, 1973, 1975, 1977, 1995
by The Lockman Foundation. Used by permission.

The author of this workbook can be contacted at chad@booksbychad.com.

Cover design by Larissa Lynch

Introduction to *Hebrews*

Hebrews is unquestionably a unique and one of the most important epistles of the New Testament (NT). It may be difficult for us to appreciate all that this book has to offer, since we cannot envision the doctrine of Christ's redemption without it. While admittedly intimidating at first, this book provides a great treasure of insight and information to the work of Christ. One who digs deep into this profound work becomes a much more enlightened disciple; he can hardly come away from it untouched and unchanged.

Hebrews takes us where few other inspired writings ever venture: deep into the heart of Christ's role as both King and High Priest. The entire epistle radiates with glowing respect for Jesus' lordship and intercession. It gives us rare glimpses into Christ's role as an obedient Son as well as His incalculable offering as the Redeemer of sinful men. Yet while the writer of *Hebrews* teaches us to adore the Savior, he also forces us to examine our own heart and where we stand with the Lord. Just as he warned his fellow Christians against succumbing to unbelief, so we today must struggle against this same temptation. Those who do not appreciate what Christ has done (and continues to do), or are ignorant of the dangers of unbelief, put themselves in danger of falling away from the truth.

Authority and Authorship: Regarding its content and authenticity, *Hebrews* has rarely been held as anything but sacred and divinely inspired. From the earliest historical assemblage of what we now refer to as the NT, this book has invariably been regarded as part of the apostolic-approved body of writings (known as the canon) that defines Christian theology and practices. Its doctrines never contradict any of those expressed elsewhere in the NT. Its style—including its reverence, intelligence, authoritativeness, majesty, etc.—is comparable to other established sacred writings, and often exceeds them. When coupled with the other facts concerning this book, such characteristics provide substantial internal evidence for its credibility. Regarding external evidence, *Hebrews* is quoted verbatim by several of the early church "fathers" who accepted it as a legitimate and primary source of Christian doctrine. It is found in nearly all (and in the oldest) versions and manuscripts of the NT, some of which date back to the second century—and possibly even the first century.

In the earliest compilations of the NT, men placed *Hebrews* between *Romans* and *Corinthians*; in one manuscript, it is between *2 Thessalonians* and *1 Timothy*. Thus, it has historically been grouped together with Paul's epistles. This would seem to indicate that Paul is its author, but this is difficult to prove. Even the early "fathers" disagreed amongst themselves on this. Some commonly suggested alternative authors include Luke, Barnabas, Apollos, or someone of such caliber as these men.[1] R.C.H. Lenski flatly dismisses Paul as the author, but then makes a rather dubious case for either the apostle James or John.[2] The scholar Simon Kistemaker seems to shrug, "I don't know," but then says, "In the final analysis, authorship is not important. The content of the epistle is what matters."[3] While this answer may not be satisfactory, it is probably the best and most honest response, given the lack of information we have regarding authorship. We will pursue some further exploration on this subject for the sake of objectivity, but in the end, each person must come to his own conclusions regarding this matter.

Some believe Paul is the author of *Hebrews* because of its rabbinic scholarliness, and he certainly was a rabbinic scholar. Indeed, whoever wrote *Hebrews* reveals his mastery of Old Testament (OT) themes and concepts, as well as NT Christology (i.e., the doctrines of the nature and work of Christ). Paul, a trained rabbi *and* inspired apostle, is indeed a qualified candidate for this work. This letter is directed exclusively to

---

1   Neil R. Lightfoot gives a detailed list of (and accompanying reasons for or against) the various authors that have been put forward over time (*Jesus Christ Today: A Commentary on the Book of Hebrews* [Abilene, TX: Bible Guides, 1976]), 19-27.

2   R. C. H. Lenski, *Commentary on the New Testament: The Interpretation of the Epistle to the Hebrews and of the Epistle of James* (Grand Rapids: Hendrickson Publishers, 1998), 8.

3   Simon J. Kistemaker, *The New Testament Commentary: Exposition of Thessalonians, the Pastorals and Hebrews* (Grand Rapids: Baker Books, 1996), 8.

a Jewish Christian audience, and yet some Jews struggled with Paul's ministry to the Gentiles (see Acts 21:17–21). Therefore, some argue that Paul, who identifies himself in all his other epistles, purposely did not identify himself here to avoid any Jewish prejudices against him. While this argument makes sense, it is not conclusive and remains a theory rather than an established fact. On the other hand, Greek scholars claim that there are several stylistic and grammatical differences between *Hebrews* and Paul's epistles. This does not prevent Paul from being its author, but we cannot overlook it, either. In some Bible translations, the superscription to the letter reads, "Paul's Epistle to the Hebrews," yet these words are supplied by translators themselves and are not found in the actual manuscripts.

We might best approach the question of authorship by simply appealing to what we *do* know about the author. For example, whoever the author is:

- He was most likely a Jew himself, being so conversant and capable in discussing Jewish law, covenant, and prophecy.
- He has written in "the most perfect Greek,"[4] having a masterful command of the language and its nuances.
- He possesses a strong command of the Levitical ministry (i.e., the priestly and sacrificial system of the Law of Moses), the ministry of Christ's own redemptive sacrifice, and an intelligent comparison of the two. He is no novice disciple; he speaks with authority, clarity, and purpose; he is a master communicator. He also speaks transcendently, that is, he looks beyond the present order of things (e.g., 12:1-3) and sees the great scope of God's deliverance through Jesus Christ as well as the human struggle with fear, doubt, and endurance.
- He is well-versed in the Septuagint, the Greek translation of the OT (completed ca. 200 BC), as this is the source of all Scripture quotes in *Hebrews*. It is significant that he would rely upon this translation (as Paul does in, say, *Romans*) in writing to Jews versus citing from the original Hebrew Bible. This implies that the Jews to whom he

---

4   Lenski, *Interpretation*, 9.

is writing are Hellenized (i.e., raised, educated, and cultured in a Greek-speaking society).
- ❏ He speaks of (or with a view toward) the termination of the old (Mosaic or Levitical) system. The primary thesis of this epistle is the superiority of Christ—His sacrifice and its implications—to the Law of Moses and its priesthood. The writer not only has a solid grasp of this transition but provides an irrefutable argument against returning to this ancient system. It is evident that he wrote during a time when non-Christian Jews still honored this system (see 13:10–14), yet it was about to be ended (8:13). Considering this, the "day" drawing near (10:25) may be an ominous reference to the coming destruction of Jerusalem (AD 70), which would permanently end any legitimate practice of the Law or its sacrifices.
- ❏ He does not speak as the founder of the congregation(s) to whom he writes, but as a minister in the field, so to speak. Nonetheless, he writes with authority and passionate conviction: he demands to be heard. He implies that their original leaders (elders and/or teachers) may have died (13:7), since their present ones are distinguished from them.[5] This indicates a well-established group of older first-generation believers mixed with second- and third-generation believers, "a group of Jewish Christians who had never seen or heard Jesus in person, but learned of Him (as the writer of the epistle also did) from some who had themselves listened to Him."[6] The epistles that we know were authored by Paul were written primarily for first-generation believers.
- ❏ He is a friend of Timothy (13:23), and a well-known teacher to those to whom he writes (13:19). However, he speaks of circumstances which are not described in any of Paul's personal letters to Timothy himself.
- ❏ He is either writing to friends (brethren) in Italy or is writing from Italy to friends who know these same people in Italy: "Those from [or "of"] Italy greet you" (13:24). Several commentators seem to interpret this to mean that the author is writing to saints in Rome;

---

5   Lenski, *Interpretation*, 11.

6   F. F. Bruce, *Commentary on the Epistle to the Hebrews* (Grand Rapids: Wm. B. Eerdmans Publishing Co., 1964), xxx).

however, this cannot be determined conclusively.
- "The author was a second-generation Christian, well versed in the study of the Septuagint [i.e., the Greek translation of the Hebrew Bible], which he interpreted according to a creative exegetical principle. He had a copious vocabulary and was a master of a fine rhetorical style, completely different from Paul's..."[7]

If *Hebrews* was written by Paul, then it would have to be written before AD 64, the generally accepted year of his death. The imminent destruction of the Jewish system, the epistle being directed to an older generation of believers, and the struggles that the writer addresses which are common to such people do seem to favor an AD 60s time of writing.[8] However, despite piecing together all the evidence available to us, we still cannot know for certain its date of composition, except that it preceded the Jewish revolts against Rome (AD 66 – 70).

Just because *Hebrews* may not have been written by Paul (or another apostle) does not mean that it is not apostolic in nature, sanctioned with apostolic authority, or uninspired by the Holy Spirit. The doctrinal content of the epistle nowhere contradicts what the apostles have written; in fact, it concurs beautifully with (particularly) Paul's and Peter's writings. It is also consistent with what is taught in the Law of Moses, without relying on rabbinical traditions, non-canonical writings (i.e., the Apocrypha), or other uninspired sources. Everything the writer explains concerning the Law or its functions (i.e., priesthood, tabernacle,

---

7   Bruce, *Commentary*, xlii.

8   David McClister warns against assuming the temple "still standing" expression (9:8) means that *Hebrews* was written prior to the destruction *of* that temple, because "Judaism did not cease to exist after the temple's destruction" (*A Commentary on Hebrews* [Temple Terrace, FL: Florida College Press, 2010], 42). While his point is true, it seems unnecessary. Just because Judaism, as a *religion*, continued after the destruction of the temple (in AD 70) does not mean that the practice of Judaism which necessarily *included* the temple and its offerings continued, because it most certainly did not and could not. The *Hebrews* writer clearly refers to Judaism as a fully functional religion, not one impaired by the absence of its central components (i.e., the temple and its priesthood). The Levitical priesthood was impossible to maintain without a temple, just as the temple was impossible to maintain without its designated priesthood.

offerings, etc.) can be ascertained through OT Scripture. Furthermore, the fact that early Christians quoted heavily from *Hebrews* alongside their quotes from Paul and other inspired writers indicates that they believed all such writings carried equal authority. Even John, an apostle who lived and wrote many years after *Hebrews* had been circulated, never contradicted or refuted this writing, even though a primary reason for his own epistles was to disprove heresies and apostasies.

Who Were the Hebrews? The ancient manuscripts from which we derive the NT offer no official title for this epistle. Yet the fact that it was written to Hebrews (Jewish Christians) is obvious.[9] Its recipients were not newcomers to the faith; the epistle is not designed to teach one how to become a Christian. These people had been faithfully teaching, practicing, and supporting the gospel for some time, but had become very discouraged over what they perceived was a lethal assault against the church. In other words, they perceived an overthrow of the church by means of external persecution, and thus were seriously considering reverting back to the only thing they knew prior to Christianity: Judaism. The several statements implying this, and the fact that the author freely appeals to Hebrew Scripture, implies that the older recipients of this letter were once immersed in the Jewish system. At the time of writing, that system is still in their blood, so to speak.[10] James Coffman describes their situation graphically:

---

9   This is "obvious" because: 1) the authority of the Old Testament (Hebrew Bible) is used without reservation or explanation; 2) the readers are understood to be well-versed in the Old Testament; 3) there are virtually no indications of a Gentile (non-Jewish) reading audience; and 4) this premise has been generally accepted since the early church fathers (2nd and 3rd century).

10 In fact, there is no proof that they had left *all* of it behind. It is likely that they still embraced much of the Jewish culture and wanted to still identify as "Hebrews" as well as (or possibly *more* than?) identifying as *Christians*. McClister, for one, argues that these Hebrews were not going to "turn back to" Judaism as much as turn *away* from Christ (*Commentary*, 26-31). However one wishes to tell the story, it appears to come out the same: *Hebrews* is about Hebrew Christians who are torn in their allegiance between Judaism and Christianity (or, the Law of Moses and Christ), and are considering abandoning one for the other. The *Hebrews* writer's purpose is to reveal which of these two deserves their *full* allegiance.

A generation had passed, and Christ had not come. The early enthusiasm inevitably generated by a new movement had begun to wane; savage persecutions had been endured; and the disciples were struggling with the problems of sin and ignorance. Moreover, they had to endure the arrogances and utter scorn of their fellow-countrymen, who taunted them with their exclusion from the old rituals, and who, out of hatred for the new faith, had launched a counter-campaign to reinlist [sic] the disciples in the fold of Judaism. After all, Judaism had indeed been founded by God himself; the glorious services of the temple reached back for a millennium or more; the old covenant had been ordained in the hands of angels; the temple itself was one of the wonders of the world; and its high priest was a powerful and respected figure in the social and political arena of those days. ... All of the traditional power of the Hebrew religion, the social excellence of its priests, the liturgical richness of the impressive ceremonial, together with the reverence of the sacred Scriptures in their custody, and all of the passionate patriotism which pertained to the old ways and concepts—all these things exerted persuasive influence over the community of Christians then struggling with manifold trials.[11]

Thus, the overall objective of *Hebrews* is to prick their conscience and remind them of their commitment to Christ, especially since everything He offers is superior to anything they had left behind.

The next logical question, then, would be: *which* Jewish Christians—in what city or area? "The common, and the almost universally received opinion is that the epistle was addressed to the Hebrew Christians in Palestine."[12] Unfortunately, this cannot be known with any certainty. The fact that the writer consistently quotes from the Septuagint (Greek translation of the Hebrews Bible) rather than the Hebrew text itself (our

---

11   James B. Coffman, *Commentary on Hebrews* (Austin, TX: Firm Foundation, 1971), 12-13.

12   Albert Barnes, *Barnes' Notes*, vol XIII (Grand Rapids: Baker Book House, no date), "Introduction."

"Old Testament") speaks to the contrary. Likely these Jews/Hebrews were Hellenized, which was not unusual for Jews outside of Judea.

In the end, the answer to this question really does not matter, since knowing the specific region to which these Jews belonged does not affect the purpose of the epistle. *Hebrews* does not specifically identify the persecution mentioned above, nor is it clear who these persecutors were: Jews or Romans.[13] The writer mentions how some had endured "the seizure of your property" (10:34), which is something expected of Roman persecution, not Jewish. If true, this would lean us toward a date of writing after Emperor Nero's persecution of the church in AD 64, when the burning of Rome was blamed upon Christians.[14] There are other subtle hints in the text that point toward a state-sanctioned persecution rather than a religious one (by the Jews). These will be given attention as we come across them in the text.

Theme and Purpose: A dominant theme of *Hebrews* is the supremacy of Christ over the Levitical system (i.e., the priesthood and sacrificial system defined by the Law of Moses). For example, we read of:

❑ **the supremacy of Christ in God's plan of redemption for man.** This is mentioned elsewhere (e.g., Eph. 1:9-10, 19-23, Col. 1:15-18, etc.), but nowhere is the idea as powerfully and eloquently developed as it is in *Hebrews*.

---

13 First, by "Romans," I do not mean literally people in Rome but those who are acting with Roman authority. Second, it is possible that the persecution came from Jews who treated Jewish Christians as heretics, as we see in the book of *Acts* (McClister, *Commentary*, 23-24). In my opinion, *Hebrews* was written later than *Acts*. The charges that the Jews brought against Paul, accusing him (before Roman governors) that Christianity was a new and therefore illegal religion in the Roman Empire, may well have taken root. The Romans had gotten used to tolerating the Jews, but Jewish Christians were seen by both parties as a heretical split from mainstream Judaism. Regardless, the real issue in *Hebrews* is not who is persecuting the Hebrew Christians but these Christians' second-guessing their allegiance to Christ.

14 It must be understood, however, that Nero's persecution was brief, particularly aimed at Christians in Rome (and vicinities), and thus relatively limited. Unlike persecutions that followed, Nero never instituted an imperial decree against all Christians everywhere or a systematic assault against the church.

- **the supremacy of Christ to Moses.** For 1,500 years, the Jews had put their faith in Moses as the foremost religious authority on earth. The very thought of anyone challenging him was abhorrent to them (see John 9:28-29). But this epistle shows Christ to be *infinitely superior* to Moses the man <u>and</u> the Law which bears his name. This is not a new challenge (see John 5:39-47, Acts 3:22-23, etc.), but one which is argued powerfully and thoroughly.
- **the supremacy of Christ to the Levitical priesthood.** The writer of *Hebrews* defines Jesus as our "great high priest who has passed through the heavens" (4:14). His priesthood bears similarity to Aaron's, the first high priest under the Law, but supersedes it in every way. Instead of merely inheriting a priesthood handed down from and corrupted by men, Christ became an entirely new High Priest of an entirely new order—one based not on a law given to men but upon God's divine oath. As a result, He has become for all believers the High Priest that neither Aaron nor any of his descendants could become.[15]
- **the supremacy of Christ's blood (life) to that of the ancient sacrifices under the Law.** Animal blood served a purpose in educating Israel in atonement for sin through sacrifice. Yet this kind of blood could not fulfill what God required for the cleansing of a human soul. Christ's blood does fulfill this, however, and is thus the most valuable substance of all time and in the entire universe. All the rivers of blood created by the sacrifices of hundreds of thousands of animals never accomplished what the shedding of Christ's blood on the cross did. *Hebrews* helps us to appreciate this from a legal standpoint and on a spiritual level that are unprecedented elsewhere in Scripture.
- **the supremacy of God's covenant with Christians.** God purposely

---

15 "It is because of his concentration on the priestly aspect of Christ's work that our author has so much to say of His death and exaltation, but so little of His resurrection. The two principal moments in the great sin-offering of Old Testament times were the shedding of the victim's blood in the court of the sanctuary and the presentation of its blood inside the sanctuary. In the antitype these two moments were seen to correspond to the death of Christ on the cross and His appearance at the right hand of God. In this pattern the resurrection, as generally proclaimed in the apostolic preaching, finds no separate place" (Bruce, *Commentary*, lvi).

and inherently limited what His covenant with Israel could do. It was not an end in itself but pointed forward to a "better covenant," one which was made effective through the blood of Christ. Those who are *now* in a covenant relationship with God ("in Christ") can approach Him with unprecedented access and with more sublime fellowship than ever before.

- **the supremacy of Christ to the ideal priest-king Melchizedek.** While this may not seem significant at first, the *Hebrews* writer develops profound conclusions based upon this comparison (7:1–28). The better we understand Melchizedek's position (Gen. 14:17–20), the more we can appreciate Christ's advocacy and authority since Christ takes this position to its highest potential.
- **Christ's supreme obedience to God.** Paul wrote of how Christ "emptied Himself" and was obedient even to the point of death on a cross (Phil. 2:7–9). The *Hebrews* writer expounds upon this even further, emphasizing the connection between His earthly obedience and eternal priesthood. Christ's obedience makes Him worthy to inaugurate a new covenant, a new priesthood, and a "new and living way" by which we can come to God (10:20).
- **Christ's supreme intercession for the believer.** Since He has been made like us—in human form yet without human corruption—Christ serves as the ideal intercessor between God and man (1 Tim. 2:5-6). Nowhere in Scripture is this doctrine so fully and magnificently developed as it is in *Hebrews*.

Beyond these details of Christ and His redemptive work, *Hebrews* expounds upon other significant perspectives closely associated with these thoughts. It teaches, for example, to:

- **learn** from the mistakes of Israel, for fear that "while a promise remains of entering His rest, any one of you may seem to have come short of it" (4:1), as what happened to an entire generation of Israelites who forfeited their opportunity to enter the Promised Land.
- **continue** to grow in maturity, not stagnating in useless "elementary" discussions, and not subsisting only on "milk" but seeking "solid

food" (5:12–13, 6:1–3). Not only are we to focus on our own spiritual growth; we are also to "stimulate" other believers to love and good deeds (10:24).
- **remember** what Christ has done for us; those who have taught us the word of God (13:7); traveling missionaries (13:2); those imprisoned for their faith (13:3); those who have exemplified the kind of faith approved by God (chapter 11); etc. Indeed, the admonition to *remember what you have been taught in Christ* consistently counters the obsolescence (or outdatedness) of the ancient (Jewish) system. Remembering Christ and His gospel is far more important than remembering 1,500 years' worth of blood offerings and law-keeping.
- **avoid unbelief** in all its forms, but particularly in *doubting Christ's pre-eminence as the Savior of all men.* Failing to believe in the Lord and His gospel will not lead to a believer's "Sabbath rest" (4:9) but God's "terrifying" judgment of him (10:31).
- **find encouragement** from the "great cloud of witnesses" (12:1), the rich legacy of faithful men and women who provide numerous examples of what it means to live by faith, even during times of great discouragement and opposition.
- **revere God** with all solemnity: "worship God with reverence and awe" (12:28) or else face the "consuming fire" which will destroy all those who do otherwise.

In sum, *Hebrews* serves as a series of admonitions to Christians. Specifically, it warned against even entertaining the thought of abandoning Christianity in favor of Judaism. In other words, believers had to make a final and absolute choice between the two belief systems. This message is just as relevant to us today: we are warned against considering (or returning to) *any* system of salvation other than Christ's since no such alternative really exists. Christ is the only Savior of men's souls (Acts 4:12); His redemption is the only redemption that God recognizes. Just as God no longer recognizes the Law of Moses as viable (for Israelites or anyone else), so He recognizes no other gospel, regardless of its claims (Gal. 1:8).

The author of *Hebrews* was obviously aware of the danger of deserting the Christian faith and the lack of appreciation that some had for Christ's sacrifice. But he does not merely offer warnings against backsliding; he also explains the *sources* of such decline. These include:

- **lack of comprehension of the big-picture perspective.** This leads to a failure to rightly discern Christ's superiority over temporary or mundane things, as well as appreciation for one's own individual participation in His church (12:25–29).
- **tendency to revert to that which is familiar but not better.** The writer of *Hebrews* defines this as "unbelief," since it implies a failure to regard Christ's gospel of redemption as credible or relevant. Such reversion (or apostasy) implies "hardness of heart" (3:8), disrespect for Christ's supreme sacrifice, and careless disregard of the Holy Spirit's sanctifying work in the heart of the believer (10:26–31).
- **spiritual ignorance resulting from a lack of careful study of Scripture (5:13 – 6:2).** By failing to educate themselves with God's inspired word (2 Tim. 3:16–17), Christians lose their "assurance" and "conviction" in Christ, the very components of faith itself (11:1–2). Such faltering, if left unchecked, inevitably leads to apostasy—the same reason ancient Israel was punished.
- **spiritual weakness (ineffectiveness) due to spiritual ignorance (12:12–13).** Christians who are ignorant of who they are and what (and who) they believe in are useless in advancing the cause of Christ. In fact, they become detrimental to the spread of this message since they wrongfully represent Christ's redemption and cause men to doubt in God's ability to save their souls.
- **forgetfulness of earlier exercises of their own great faith (10:32–39).** Just as the Ephesians lost their "first love" (Rev. 2:4), so these Christians had lost their initial zeal and commitment to the Lord.
- **forgetfulness of the "faithful" who had preceded them.** This forgetfulness isolated and disconnected these Christians from the universal perspective of God's people throughout all time, forcing them into a very narrow, pessimistic mindset. This disconnectedness is also manifested in literal abandonment of assemblies of the saints (10:25).

- **failure to appreciate the new and "unshaken kingdom."** God's kingdom under Christ's leadership will not diminish or be overthrown by any worldly power or secular government. These Christians wanted to abandon this pure and infallible kingdom for the old (Israelite) kingdom, which was fraught with human corruption and insurmountable limitations.
- **failure to see all the benefits and blessings which they had in Christ.** Instead of finding confidence in blessings and promises of God, people tend to focus on temporary setbacks and human discouragement. Since we live in a transient and physical world, we are accustomed to transient and material-world thinking. God has given us every reason to transcend such thinking, but difficulties of this life will prove to be challenging (see Mat. 13:20–22). Thus, Christians must make great effort to stay focused on the things that are spiritual and eternal rather than earthly and temporary (2 Cor. 4:16–18, Col. 3:1–4).

Finally, the writer reminds his readers that "Jesus Christ is the same yesterday and today and forever" (13:8). This statement underlies the entire epistle: since Jesus does not change, then whatever was happening to the Hebrews did not indicate a change in His gospel, or a disintegration of His power or authority. It is the Hebrew Christians *themselves* who were changing, not the Lord; *they* were the ones leaving God, even though God promised never to leave them (13:5b–6).

SECTION ONE: THE SUPREMACY OF CHRIST (1:1—3:6)

Christ Is Heir of All Things (1:1–3)

The first verses (1:1-3) acknowledge the majesty and deity of Jesus Christ, who is the subject—directly or indirectly—of this entire work. The absence of any personal introductory remarks or salutations is unique among the NT epistles. This characteristic makes *Hebrews* difficult to categorize: is it a doctrinal treatise for the church? Or is it an epistle to a particular group of Christians? Ultimately, it is both: while it begins as a treatise on the supreme nature of Christ, it concludes as a letter of exhortation to the brethren.[16]

The opening line (1:1) assumes the existence and sovereign authority of God, like what we find in *Genesis* and *John*. "He is a God who speaks; and, because only a person can speak, this reveals him as a personal God."[17] Every fact we know about God has come to us through His divine revelation. The manner of that revelation, however, has progressed as humankind matured in its understanding.[18] Thus, throughout this epistle, the writer regularly draws significant contrasts to what *was* (i.e., the Law of Moses) and what *now is* (i.e., the gospel of

---

16 "It has been said that Hebrews begins like a treatise, continues like a sermon, and concludes like a letter" (Lightfoot, *Jesus Christ Today*, 43). On the form of the book, McClister offers an excellent overview, suggesting that *Hebrews* "was a sermon in the form of a piece of literature," as it does have the rhetorical style of a sermon (compare Paul's sermon in Acts 13:15ff) (*Commentary*, 55-58).

17 Coffman, *Commentary*, 18.

18 "At the beginning of the revelation, the presentation was elementary. Later it appealed to a more developed spiritual sense. Again, the revelation differed according to the faithfulness or unfaithfulness of Israel" (Kenneth Wuest, *Word Studies from the Greek New Testament* [Grand Rapids: Eerdmans Publishing, 1947], 32).

Christ). His opening remarks already illustrate this:

Then	Now
"long ago"	"in these last days"
"in many portions and many ways"	in this one way [implied; see John 14:6]
"[God] spoke to the fathers"	"[God speaks] to us"
"in the prophets"	"in His Son"

The "last days" refer to the Christian era. The context for "last days" has to do with the manner of God's revelation to men (1 Peter 1:20-21).[19] Before Christ ("long ago"), God communicated to men in various ways: prophecies, high priests,[20] dreams, "types" (or shadows), and signs performed among Israel. Now, all essential revelation from God to man has come to us through His Son, Jesus Christ—either directly (by His own words) or indirectly (by His own apostles—see 2 Peter 3:1-2). Before, God's revelation spanned centuries through a slow unfolding and gradual disclosure. In less than a century, God revealed more than He ever had done through His prophets over centuries of time. Jesus Himself is God's supreme revelation to man: the word of God in the flesh (John 1:1-2, 14). "As God had no greater messenger than His Son, He had no further message beyond the gospel."[21]

---

19   While *specifically* "last days" could refer to the end of the Jewish Age, being finalized by the destruction of Jerusalem in AD 70, the usage here is not specific. The writer is making a general contrast between how God revealed His will to believers *then* and *now*: "then" He spoke through the Law and the prophets (Deut. 18:18-19); "now" He speaks through His Son (Mat. 17:5). The fact that He *still* speaks through His Son today (through the gospel) indicates that the "last days" are not completed but that we are still in them. There will not be yet another set of "days" in which we listen to someone other than God's Son; we are in the final revelatory age.

20   Specifically, through the Urim and Thummim ("lights and perfection"), the special breastplate worn by the high priest which was used to consult God for difficult decisions; see Exod. 28:30 and Num. 27:21.

21   Bruce, *Commentary*, 26. McClister concurs: "The fact that God has now spoken in one person (Jesus) reflects the finality of God's message through him. The new revelation was given once and for all (*cf.* Jude 3). Man needs no more revelation from God after this. The fact that the apostles received revelation after Jesus left the earth does not contradict this, because it was Jesus who was speaking through them (1 Cor.

While God was "in" the prophets of old, as they were filled with His Spirit, Jesus *is* God (i.e., a divine Being) and is filled with His Spirit "without measure" (John 3:34). God appointed Christ "heir of all things"—not simply "an" heir but the *sole* Heir (1:2)—since He is God's only begotten Son (John 3:16). He alone is the sole recipient of all His Father's wealth and power. Whatever belongs to God now belongs to Christ (Mat. 11:27, John 3:35, 16:15, etc.).[22] Christ did not take His Father's authority illegitimately, but the Father *gave* all things to Him (Mat. 28:18). He built His church with His Father's full consent and blessing. "The church is His, but all other things are likewise His, for He governs these in the interest of His church."[23]

But Christ was not powerless and without authority prior to His ascension to His Father's right hand (Acts 2:33). While we know little of Christ's pre-incarnate existence, we *do* know that all Creation came into existence through Him (see John 1:3, 1 Cor. 8:5-6, and Col. 1:15-17). He did this with the power and authority He has always possessed as God. In other words, before Christ was revealed to *us* as God's "Son," He has always existed in *heaven* as one of the Godhead. Thus, Christ's kingship was not the beginning of His power but marks a particular phase and fulfills a specific need of God's kingdom: as the Redeemer of human souls. As powerful as God the Father is, He cannot remove the sins of men by Himself. The work of God the Son was necessary to accomplish this: His sacrifice, His blood, and His intercession.[24] There is not now and never will be *anyone* comparable to Jesus Christ. He is the Creator of

---

14:37, 1 Thess. 4:2, 2 Peter 3:2)" (*Commentary*, 70).

22   The Father Himself is exempted in this transference of authority (1 Cor. 15:27-28). Even though Christ is given "all authority" (Mat. 28:18), He does not exercise authority over His Father, but the two work together as one (John 17:22-23).

23   Lenski, *Interpretation*, 35.

24   We know Christ as "God's Son" because we would not understand His relationship to the Father in any other way. He is *like* a "son" in many respects. Yet aside from His earthly existence, He is *not* like an earthly son for the following reasons: He has always existed (John 8:58); He has no mother; He possessed divine, creative power and authority even before He inherited His Father's kingdom; He never fails or disappoints His Father; and probably several other reasons. Furthermore, God the Son can die and be resurrected but God the Father cannot die, which is why God the Father could not offer *Himself* as a sacrifice for men's souls.

our world, and He is the end (or completion) of God's revelation to man. He is truly, as He claims, the "Alpha and Omega, the beginning and end" (Rev. 22:13).

Christ is not merely a reflection of God's glory: He is filled with it (1:3a; see John 1:14, Col. 1:19, and 2:9). "Exact representation" means an imprint, stamp, or essential character (of something).[25] Thus, Christ bears the *full, expressed nature* of the Father, reproducing His glory without blurring, distortion, or misinterpretation. While on earth, Christ provided an accurate portrayal of His Father who dwells in heaven (John 1:18, 10:30, and 14:7-10). Furthermore, "all things" are maintained by His omnipotence; the present infinitive tense of the verb ("He upholds...") indicates an action that is happening now and continues to happen perpetually.

Having described who Christ is, the writer now turns to what He has accomplished (1:3b). "Purification of sins" refers to the atoning sacrifice carried out on the cross. This purification was not for His sins, since He was sinless, but for ours since we cannot approach God otherwise. This describes a priestly action: our having been sprinkled with His blood (1 Peter 1:2) alludes to what was performed by the ancient Levitical priests in making atonement for sins of the sons of Israel (Lev. 1:5, 3:2, 5:6, 16:14, etc.). In this indirect manner, Christ is introduced to us as our High Priest: His is *like* the Levitical priesthood but exceeds it in every respect.

The writer then mentions another aspect of Christ's work (1:3b): "He sat down at the right hand of the Majesty on high." In the OT, the priest's work was always performed standing up, never sitting down. Priests minister, kings rule; priests work standing up (offering sacrifices), kings work sitting down (to rule on a throne). Having accomplished all things that God required of a divine High Priest, Christ then took His

---

25 This is from the Greek word *charakter* ("character") (A. T. Robertson, *Word Pictures in the New Testament*, vol. V [Grand Rapids: Baker Book House, 1960], 336; Wuest, *Word Studies*, 37-39). As one's character is the true image of who that person really is, so Christ's "character" is an exact image of the Father (John 14:7-9).

rightful place next to the Father to rule over His Father's kingdom. This necessarily implies the entire *completion* of Christ's ministry since He would never have "sat down" if more redemptive work remained (see Acts 2:33, Eph. 1:20-21, and Col. 3:1). Consider what the following passages say concerning His authority as King:

- "'The Lord said to my Lord, "Sit at My right hand, until I put Your enemies beneath Your feet."'" (Mat. 22:44)
- "Therefore having been exalted to the right hand of God, and having received from the Father the promise of the Holy Spirit, He has poured forth this which you both see and hear." (Acts 2:33)
- "He is the one whom God exalted to His right hand as a Prince and a Savior, to grant repentance to Israel, and forgiveness of sins." (Acts 5:31)
- "who is the one who condemns? Christ Jesus is He who died, yes, rather who was raised, who is at the right hand of God, who also intercedes for us." (Rom. 8:34)
- "which He brought about in Christ, when He raised Him from the dead and seated Him at His right hand in the heavenly places, far above all rule and authority and power and dominion, and every name that is named …" (Eph. 1:20-21)
- "Therefore if you have been raised up with Christ, keep seeking the things above, where Christ is, seated at the right hand of God." (Col. 3:1)
- "Now…we have such a high priest, who has taken His seat at the right hand of the throne of the Majesty in the heavens…" (Heb. 8:1)
- "but He, having offered one sacrifice for sins for all time, sat down at the right hand of God…" (Heb. 10:12)
- "fixing our eyes on Jesus, the author and perfecter of faith, who for the joy set before Him endured the cross, despising the shame, and has sat down at the right hand of the throne of God." (Heb. 12:2)
- "Corresponding to that, baptism now saves you—not the removal of dirt from the flesh, but an appeal to God for a good conscience—through the resurrection of Jesus Christ, who is at the right hand of God, having gone into heaven, after angels and authorities and powers had been subjected to Him." (1 Peter 3:21-22)

The "sitting" here is figurative but symbolizes two things: the supreme authority of Christ *and* the completion of His redemptive work here upon earth. To summarize:

- We are in the "last days" of God's revelation to man. There are no more "days" in which new or surpassing revelations will be given.
- In these "last days," God has spoken to us in His own Son: He is our final authority.
- God's Son is the exact image of His Father: if we know Christ, we know the Father.
- He (the Son) is the Creator of all that has begun to exist.
- He continues to uphold all things by the word of His sovereign power.
- He has made purification (on the cross) for the souls of men (as our High Priest).
- Having done this, He has sat down at the right hand of the Father (as our King).

Christ's Supremacy over Angels (1:3b—2:4)

A More Excellent Name than Angels (1:4-14): Perhaps the writer felt compelled to address angels' inferiority to Christ in response to angelology, the study and worship of angels that was popular among the Jewish elite in the first century (also implied in Col. 2:18). He is "better" not only in worthiness but also in rank; He has "a more excellent name than" any angel; therefore, He deserves more reverence and recognition than them. Christ's "name" indicates His authority, status (as God's Son), and all the attending privileges associated with His position (Phil. 2:9-11).

- The quotes in 1:5 are from Psalm 2:7 and 2 Sam. 7:14, respectively.[26]

---

26 Whenever the writer cites a particular verse from a psalm, it is understood (by his readers) that he refers to the entire context of the psalm. Thus, he is not "proof-texting," as is common among those who pull passages out of context in support of a pre-determined agenda. Rather, the writer here cites a sampling of the OT passage,

God never refers to any angel as His "Son" or His "Begotten"; there is no hint in Scripture of a father-son relationship between God and His angels.[27] However, Christ's sonship to the Father serves as one of the fundamental underpinnings of the gospel:

- The angel Gabriel declared to Mary, "He [Jesus] will be great and will be called the Son of the Most High …" (Luke 1:32)
- God the Father declared upon Jesus' baptism, "This is My Beloved Son, in whom I am well-pleased." (Mat. 4:17)
- Peter said (and Jesus never corrected him), "You are the Christ, the Son of the living God." (Mat. 16:16)
- "And the high priest said to Him, 'I adjure You by the living God, that You tell us whether You are the Christ, the Son of God.' Jesus said to him, 'You have said it yourself …'" (Mat. 26:63-64)

☐ The source of the quote in 1:6 is obscure. Some commentators connect it with Deut. 32:43 but having been re-worded in the Septuagint. Others identify it with Psalm 97:7—again, from the Septuagint. Regardless, no angel ever held the rank or position of pre-eminence as Christ but instead they give honor and glory to Him.

☐ The quote in 1:7 is from Psalm 104:4, which was regularly sung on Friday evenings and Saturday (Sabbath) mornings to highlight God's providential care for all the earth.[28] The writer of *Hebrews* inserted "angels" into that passage, since the word is necessarily implied. God's Son ministers as an eternal King; in great contrast, angels serve in capacities far below Him. "Winds" and "flame" indicate fleeting, non-permanent things—not the lifespan of an angel but rather to an angel's particular ministries.

---

knowing that his (Jewish) readers are going to be familiar with the entire reading. Likewise, we should familiarize ourselves with the entire psalm's context to gain this same appreciation for what is being said.

27 Someone might question this, based on passages like Job 1:6 and 2:1, where the "sons of God" presented themselves before the Lord. However, the usage and context there is so general that literal *sonship* cannot be meant. God is "Father"—thus, *life-giver*—to all living beings; thus, every living, intelligent creature is His "son." Yet angels are no more *literal* (or begotten) "sons" of God than Timothy was a literal "son" of Paul (2 Tim. 1:2).

28 Kistemaker, *NTC*, 41.

- Quotes in 1:8-9 are from Psalm 45:6-7; in 1:10-12, from Psalm 102:25-27. "The great significance of its use here [i.e., of the latter citation] is in the fact that words originally addressed to Jehovah are unhesitatingly applied to Jesus Christ."[29] No angel was ever said to occupy a "throne," given a "scepter," or "anointed" by God. These are all kingly terms that have been applied to men (such as David) but are ideally applied to Christ the King, in fulfillment of several prophecies (Gen. 49:10, 2 Sam. 7:13-16, Psalm 89:20-21, and Isa. 9:6-7). Also, no angel was ever credited with laying the foundations of the earth or with the creation of the heavens, but the Son has been credited with all of these (John 1:3, Col. 1:16-17).
- The quotation in 1:13 is from Psalm 110:1, the most-quoted psalm in the entire NT.[30] "Sitting" does not suggest idleness, but (here) just the opposite: the activity of kingly rule and authority. This might be paraphrased, "You [Son] rule on Your throne until I [Father] usher in the time in which all Your enemies will be forced to acknowledge Your glory." (See further comments on 10:13.) Christ uses this same passage with reference to Himself (Mat. 22:41-45). For a king to put his feet upon his enemies signifies complete and unconditional superiority over them (see Josh. 10:22-25). But no angel was ever promised such kingship or pre-eminence; we have no record in Scripture of angels sitting (in authority) on thrones. Angels are *authorized* by God to do or say certain things but are never given their own authority as Christ possesses.
- Angels are not the *object* of God's concern but are instead employed as servants to "render service for the sake of those who will inherit salvation" (1:14). Angels serve the King (Christ) but are never compared to Him; likewise, Christ is never referred to as an angel. At the same time, angels are never used for preaching the gospel to men; that is a work limited only to Christ, His Spirit, and His followers on earth.[31] The Son alone has unique and unprecedented

---

29 Coffman, *Commentary*, 32; bracketed words are mine.

30 Psalm 110:1 has been cited or referred to by Jesus (Luke 20:43), Peter (Acts 2:35), Paul (1 Cor. 15:25), and elsewhere by the *Hebrews* writer (5:6, 7:17,21, 10:13, etc.).

31 Lenski, *Interpretation*, 62.

honor; no angel can compare to him. And if no *angel* can share honor with Him, then certainly no *man*—not even Moses—can be honored alongside Him, either.

The Superiority of What Christ Said (2:1-4): Having established Christ's supremacy to angels, the writer now shows the necessary implications of this (2:1). Since Christ is greater than heavenly angels, what He has revealed (His gospel) is greater than whatever revelation came through angels (the Law of Moses). This superior message deserves "much closer attention" than what was given to Israel. To "drift away" calls to mind a boat carried away by the tide because the anchor was not properly set. It is not the result of willful rebellion but carelessness and inattention.

The "word" (in 2:2) refers specifically to God's covenant with Israel, which was "spoken" or commanded through angels (see Acts 7:53 and Gal. 3:19). While there is no literal reference to angels speaking the Law to Moses, this has been the mode of God's presentation of Himself to people in ancient times.[32] The contrast between how the Law was presented and how Christ's gospel was presented is in how both laws were communicated: one, by angelic intercession; the other, "in His Son" (recall 1:2). Angels were never the source of authority for divine commandments; Christ, however, *is* the source of authority for His teaching (Mat. 7:29, 28:19).

The Law of Moses was binding upon Israel, and disobedience to it warranted serious consequences, including execution. If a law ordained by angels is authoritative and binding, then "how will we escape" divine condemnation for disregarding a "so great a salvation" as ordained by Christ Himself—One who is higher than *all* angels (2:3a)? Christ confirmed this message first by His own authority, in anticipation of its

---

32 First, consider the several references to the "angel of the Lord" in God's communication with men (as in Exod. 3:2). Second, the pillar of cloud (or fire) is referred to in this same way (Exod. 14:19, 32:34). Third, an "angel of the Lord" would lead Israel into battle against the Canaanites (Exod. 23:20, 33:2). The point is: God has used angels throughout the revelation of His law to His people, indicating that the Law, though revealed to earthly men, was of heavenly origin.

being put into effect. His gospel—the *new* covenant—could not have been put into effect without blood (His death) and His legitimate place at the right hand of God (His enthronement). Even so, He demonstrated His divine nature through His teaching, fulfillment of ancient prophecies, His Father's own admission, numerous miracles, and even Moses' own testimony (see John 5:31-47).

This gospel was also confirmed by "those who heard" Christ. Most notably, this would be His apostles (2:3b) but may include other preachers as well (Luke 1:1-2). This statement also implies that the writer along with his main audience belongs to a second generation of believers.[33] God Himself "testifying with them [i.e., eyewitnesses of Christ]" refers directly to God's audible affirmation that Jesus was indeed His Son (Mat. 4:17, 17:5, and John 12:28) and therefore spoke with divine authority. Thus, the apostles testified by their own eyewitness accounts (2 Peter 3:1-2, 1 John 1:1-3) and God underscored their testimony with His own.

Finally, this new covenant message—superior to the one ordained by angels in every respect—was confirmed by far more, far different, and far greater miracles than even what Israel had seen at the inauguration of their own covenant. Christ performed "signs and wonders and… various miracles," as did His apostles (compare John 5:36, 10:37-38, Acts 1:3, and 2 Cor. 12:12). These demonstrations of supernatural power provided irrefutable proof of the authority of the message *and* the One who gave it (Luke 4:36, John 3:2). These signs culminated in Christ's resurrection from the dead—a resurrection that, unlike other resurrections (Acts 9:37-41, 20:8-12, etc.), had no human involvement or intercession. Such signs could not be ignored or explained away; even Christ's detractors could not deny them (John 11:47, Acts 4:16, etc.).

As an extension of the signs performed by Christ and His apostles, the Holy Spirit—the power behind *all* signs and wonders—gave "gifts [or, distributions]" to certain believers for the purpose of confirming that the

---

33 According to some, it also indicates that *Hebrews* was not written by one of the apostles; see Kistemaker, *NTC*, 59; Lenski, *Interpretation*, 68; etc.

things being taught and done in Christ's church were in fact approved by God (2:4). The Spirit provided these spiritual gifts "for the common good" (1 Cor. 12:7, 28) until the time when the written word would be the only proof necessary to confirm Christ's gospel.

The Law of Moses was from heaven, being ordained by angels; the gospel is also from heaven but is ordained by the Son of God. The gospel, then, supersedes whatever had gone before it since Christ supersedes every angel in heaven: His divine nature is superior to the created nature of angels. By implication, this also means that those seeking God cannot pursue anything *less* than the gospel of God's Son. This is a major thesis statement of this epistle.

Christ's Supremacy over Humankind (2:5–18)

God Subjected the Earth to Men (2:5-8): Having established that Christ has supremacy over all angels, the writer now turns his attention to His relationship with humankind. His use of "world" here (in 2:5) means literally "the inhabited earth"; "to come" refers to that age after the word of God was communicated by angels (Heb 2:2).[34] Thus, the writer simply means the Christian age, for it is this of "which we are speaking."[35] "He means by 'the world to come' the Christian world-order, the glorious era of salvation inaugurated by the Messiah and pressing on toward consummation at His second coming—the new order which by its very existence renders obsolete the prior dispensation."[36]

---

34 "The author is discussing this new order introduced by Christ which makes obsolete the old dispensation of rites and symbols. God did not put this new order in charge of angels" (Robertson, *Word Pictures*, 344).

35 Some (such as Premillennialists) wish to use this passage as "proof" that Christians will live forever in a rehabilitated, glorified earth. Yet one must impose a considerable amount of imagination into this text to arrive at such conclusions. The context here deals with man's earthly dominion as it presently stands (Gen. 1:26-30), with a view toward the *perfection* of earthly types and foreshadows in heaven. Just as the body must die because of sin (Rom. 8:10), so the physical system must be put to death (i.e., ended) for the same reason. This sin-corrupted world will not be a part of the church's glorified future (Rev. 21:1-2).

36 Lightfoot, *Jesus Christ Today*, 72.

In other words, while angels were used to communicate with men in the ancient world, the "world to come" (in comparison to the ancient world) is overseen by Christ, even though the physical world was put in subjection to men, not angels.

The quote from Psalm 8:4-6 (in 2:6-7) does not speak of Christ, as many assume, but of mortal men. Men are "for a little while lower than the angels" in *glory* and *proximity* to God (2:6-8).[37] While angels now behold the face of God (Luke 1:19, Mat. 18:10), we have no such privilege. We have received "glory and honor" in an earthly context but not in full. Nonetheless, the gospel promises that people will also receive dominion over the future world with Christ (Mat. 19:28-29, Rev. 3:21, etc.). At that time, believers will reign *over* angels (1 Cor. 6:2-3).[38] The "all things in subjection under his [man's] feet" phrase recalls 1:13, in which Jesus' enemies will acknowledge their subjection to Him. Christ is a forerunner for the faithful who will share in His glory.

In the beginning, God put the entire earth in subjection to man (Gen. 1:29-30, 9:1-3, Isa. 45:18, etc.). When Adam sinned, he brought a curse upon himself that negatively affected his (and his posterity's) relationship with the earth (Gen. 3:17-19). In other words, things are not *now* as God originally intended. "We do not yet see all things subjected to him [man]" (2:8b)—that is, the physical, earthly system has not yet been fulfilled and the future realm has not yet been visibly disclosed to us. Man was made to be a master of this world but instead made himself a slave to sin (Gen. 4:7, John 8:34, Rom. 6:16, etc.), and the natural world suffers because of this.

---

37 The Greek word for "man" in this passage (2:6) is not *aner* (male) but *anthropos* (a generic term for a human being), in reference to mankind (Wuest, *Word Studies*, 56.)

38 Robert Milligan strongly disagrees: "I know of no evidence in the Scriptures that the present rank of men and angels will ever be reversed" (*The New Testament Commentary*, vol IX [Delight, AR: Gospel Light], 86). Yet, the gospel speaks of us reigning with Christ (2 Tim. 2:12, etc.), and if Christ reigns over the angels, then we will also reign over the angels. Likewise, Christ will share His inheritance with His redeemed (Eph. 1:13-14) and not with angels. We are beneath them "for a little while" but not forever.

Jesus Also Was Made "Lower than the Angels" (2:9-18): "But we do see..." (2:9)—i.e., while we do not yet see in ourselves or our world the full scope of what God had intended for us, in Christ we *do* see this. Because of His perfect life on earth, He now has been "crowned with glory and honor" in heaven (Phil. 2:9). In His role as the Son of Man, Christ was *also* "for a little while lower than the angels" (when He "became flesh"—John 1:14) so He could identify with and thus intercede for us. While having taken on an earthly, carnal existence, He maintained His authority over all the angels. In fact, throughout the gospels, we see angels ministering *to* Jesus, never wielding authority *over* Him (Mat. 4:6, 11, 26:53, Luke 22:43, and John 1:51). Thus, in His case, "lower than the angels" has to do with His human nature, not His divine authority. In becoming a Man, He never ceased to be the divine Son of God. Coffman says concerning this passage:

> This verse emphasizes the differences between man's potential and what he has actually become. The grave consequences of the fall of Adam, the expulsion from Eden, the cursing of the ground, and the imposition of the penalty of death—all these things have for long ages frustrated the human attainment of the purpose of God in man. Instead of all things being in subjection to him, man finds that he cannot even control himself; and beyond that there are countless things that he cannot subdue or subject to himself, so much so that unaided humanity must ever despair of any true realization of the royal dominion assigned in Genesis 1. But Jesus Christ came, taking upon Him the form of a servant, providing for the plenary [full or complete—MY WORDS] discharge of man's sin, tasting of death for every man, and rising to heaven with man's glorified nature upon Him, and thus on man's behalf achieving that dominion of man intended from the beginning.[39]

As a man, Jesus could not have descended any lower than His death upon the cross. In that death, He exercised humility incomprehensible to us, as we have never seen the glory that He surrendered to do this (Phil.

---

39   Coffman, *Commentary*, 49.

2:5-9). Jesus overcame this world, sin, death, and every other obstacle that stood in the way of our attaining full fellowship with the Father. That He "[tasted] death" for everyone (2:9) does not mean merely that Jesus died, for every person "tastes death" in that sense. But for the Son of God to "taste [or, experience] death" speaks to the *full importance* of His sacrificial death: what it signified, what it accomplished, what it overcame. The author implies rhetorically: What (other) man has accomplished this? What angel? What *law*? The Law of Moses, as sacred as it was, could not redeem those who transgressed it (Acts 13:38-39); its sacrifices, as plentiful as they were, could not atone for a single sin (Heb. 10:4). Yet through His supreme act of self-sacrifice, Christ can justify the transgressor, having secured full atonement for his sins (Rom. 3:23-24).

The Law of Moses, though ordained by angels and ratified by animal blood, was still unable to do what Christ accomplished through His death (2:10-13). It appears at first that God is the initial "He" mentioned in 2:10, but this seems inconsistent with what has been said so far. The *Hebrews* writer has already spoken of Christ as the One through whom and for whom all things have been made (recall 1:2). Thus, the Creator gave Himself up for His Creation; nothing *less* than this kind of sacrifice could have atoned for the sin *of* the Creation. Christ made *Himself* the "author" [lit., leader; captain; pioneer] of salvation through His own suffering.[40] He was "perfected" through His offering in that His sufferings fulfilled the objective of God's plan of redemption for man (e.g., Isa. 53:10 and Col. 1:19-20). Through His sufferings, "many sons" (faithful believers) are saved. He is the "author of salvation" in that He defines the terms of His saving gospel, just as He defines the faith God requires of those saved by it (Heb. 12:2).

Since Christ has so identified with man, even having endured unspeakable suffering for his sake, "He is not ashamed to call them [believers] brethren" (2:11). Christ the Sanctifier and those who are

---

40 "The Greek word (*archegos*) denotes a leader of one who initiates something, one who is first, who goes before others and makes their passage possible" (McClister, *Commentary*, 107). The same word is used in 12:2 as well as in Acts 3:15 and 5:31.

sanctified are all from one Father: as Christ was sent from the Father, so we derive spiritual life from the Father. (The OT quotes in 2:12-13 are from Psalm 22:22 and Isa. 8:17-18.) As Jesus trusted in God, He therefore gladly represents those who also trust in Him—namely, God's sons in the faith (Gal. 3:26). As God's only begotten Son, Christ is our Brother as well as our Lord: He identifies with us intimately and compassionately.

Jesus so *completely* identifies with us that He became "flesh and blood" as we are (2:14-16). In doing so, He did not abandon His divine nature: He became the one (human) without ceasing to be the other (deity) (John 1:14). The *purpose* for this was to rescue "the children" (i.e., faithful believers) from the grip of fear and death (Col. 1:12-14). "The only way He could deal with death was by dying, and the only way He could die was by becoming human."[41] As Christ represents "His brethren" before God, so we represent Him before men; as Christ and "His brethren" have a common existence (in the flesh), so we have a common enemy: Satan. As Jesus defeated Satan, so we overcome him through Jesus (Mat. 12:29, John 16:33). As David cut off Goliath's head with the giant's own sword, Jesus destroyed the devil's works with his own weapon: death (1 John 3:8). At the same time, our knowledge of this "death" is limited since none of us has experienced it. "Until we understand perfectly what death is, we cannot of course fully understand its power."[42]

The "slavery" here (2:15) is the insurmountable burden of trying to achieve righteousness through law-keeping or human effort (Gal. 5:1-4). It is the *pronouncement* of death and *anticipation* of punishment for having sinned against God. Satan has no authority to cast souls into hell, but he has long accused sinners of being unworthy of God's atonement. He induces people to sin, incapacitates them with guilt, and capitalizes

---

41   Robert Jamieson, Andrew Fausset, and David Brown, *Commentary Critical and Explanatory on the Whole Bible (1871)*, electronic edition (database © 2012 by WORDsearch Corp.), on 2:14. Bruce says: "In order to be a perfect high priest, a man must sympathize with those on whose behalf he acts, and he cannot sympathize with them unless he can enter into their experiences and share them for himself" (*Commentary*, 44).

42   Milligan, *Commentary*, 99.

on their fear of judgment. He deceives sinners into believing they can achieve righteousness apart from God's grace. "To sin is to enter into a bitter slavery under a hard taskmaster (Satan), a slavery from which there is no human remedy and that will result in the slave's death (John 8:34, Rom. 6:16)."[43]

Yet Christ has removed all Satan's threats: His blood cleanses us from all sin (1 John 1:7) and therefore spares us from the punishment for sin. Now that enlightened with divine truth, we no longer are to be seduced by Satan's deceptions. Where Satan enslaves and imprisons, Christ liberates (John 8:31-32). Having "abolished death" (2 Tim. 1:10), He has imparted life and peace with God (Rom. 5:1-2). Christ offers no salvation to angels, but only to "His brethren" (2:16).[44] The "descendant of Abraham" refers to the children of God who, like Abraham, are justified by their faith *in* God (Rom. 4:22-24, Gal. 3:6-9, and 3:26-29).

Based on this passage (2:15-16) and others, Satan has been defeated, yet he still maintains a measure of power, influence, and control over people. This can be confusing to Christians who do not understand the context of his defeat. Satan has not been *removed from the picture* since we are still told to be on guard for his schemes (2 Cor. 2:11) and that he is still a threat to us (1 Peter 5:8). Some believe that Satan has been completely neutralized (often citing Rev. 20:1-3, a visionary scene) and that what we are experiencing today is merely "residual evil" from what he sowed from many centuries before.

Yet the NT gives a different picture—one that should not be ignored. Satan most certainly has been defeated by Christ through His death: He came to "destroy the works of the devil" (1 John 3:8) and He overcame Satan's *powers*. But this language refers to the "works" and powers that

---

43   McClister, *Commentary*, 113.

44   The reason for this is because all salvation from sin is obtained through faith in God—a faith that has not yet seen the One who saves but believes in Him (Heb. 11:1-2, 6). Angels that sin, however, have already dwelt in the presence of God and therefore cannot exercise faith: no one needs faith (or hope) for what he has already seen (Rom. 8:24-25). Instead of being offered salvation, angels that sin are simply condemned and await a future judgment (2 Peter 2:4, Jude 1:6).

Satan has over believers who have chosen to draw near to God (James 4:7-8). By severing our allegiance to Satan in our baptism into Christ, we rob him of his full power over us and allow Christ to lead us instead. (This is not an unchangeable situation: Christians still have the right to choose—even very unwisely—whom they will serve.) It does not mean that Satan has been eliminated from the great cosmic drama of human life—not yet anyway.[45]

To become our "merciful and faithful high priest," Christ had to personally identify with those for whom He intercedes (2:17-18). The high priest's primary responsibility was to minister to the "things pertaining to God," and especially in making "propitiation" for sinners.[46] "Propitiation" is the act of appeasing God's wrath through blood sacrifice; it seeks God's mercy in the place of His judgment.[47] This is the first direct mention of Jesus' high-priestly role, yet this subject will be discussed throughout much of this epistle from here forward.[48] Thus, we would do well to familiarize ourselves with the different aspects of the Levitical high priest which foreshadow the perfection of Christ's high-priestly role:

---

45 For more information on "the darkness," Satan, and Christ's victory over him, I strongly recommend my book, *This World Is Not Your Home* (Spiritbuilding Publishers, 2022); go to www.spiritbuilding.com/chad.

46 This alludes to the Levitical high priest's role in the Day of Atonement (Lev. 16), in which atonement was made for the entire nation of Israel. The student of *Hebrews* would do well to read and become well-acquainted with that event. The writer not only draws on it heavily throughout his epistle, but the Day of Atonement ritual also serves as a primitive yet effective illustration of Christ's mediatory role for His church.

47 "Propitiation" (2:17; see Rom. 3:25, 1 John 2:2, and 4:10) alludes to the OT use of the word "covering," the same as is used to describe the lid [lit., mercy seat] of the ark of the covenant. Synonyms include "expiation," "satisfaction," and "atonement."

48 "High priest" is used 17 times in *Hebrews* in reference to Christ, but nowhere else in the NT is He referred to in this way.

Levitical high priest	Christ as the eternal High Priest
Pure lineage: from the tribe of Levi *and* the family of Aaron (Exod. 28:41-43)	*Pure lineage:* Son of God *and* the Son of Man—specifically, a descendant of David, according to promise (2 Sam. 7:8-16, Rom. 1:1-4)
Pure body: no one could serve who had some physical defect (Lev. 21:16-23)	*Pure body:* no bones broken (John 19:31-37), no physical defect that would disqualify Him from serving as High Priest (Luke 2:52)
Pure relationships (Lev. 21:13-15)	*Pure relationships:* sinless in all His dealings with people (1 Peter 2:22); not defiled with any unholy unions (2 Cor. 6:14-16)
Dedicated to the Lord (Exod. 28:36-38, Lev. 21:11-13)	*Dedicated to the Lord:* "consumed" with His Father's work (John 2:16-17; see also John 5:17, Mark 10:45, Heb. 10:7, etc.)
Wore garments appropriate for his office (Exod. 28:1ff)	*Wore garments appropriate for His office:* symbolized in Rev. 1:12-16, implying His holy works (as required also of believers; see Rev. 19:7-8)
Anointed with the holy oil (Lev. 8:10-12)	*Anointed with God's Spirit* (Psalm 89:20, Mat. 4:16-17, Luke 4:18-19, and Acts 4:27)
Interceded (made propitiation) for the sins of Israel with sacrifices and blood (Lev. 16)	*Interceded (made propitiation) for all sinners with His own body and blood* (Eph. 1:7, 1 Peter 2:24, Heb. 10:10, etc.)
Blessed the nation with benedictions (Num. 6:22-26)	*Blesses the church with spiritual blessings* (Gal. 3:9,14, Eph. 1:3)
Upon his death, Israelites who lived under the sentence of death were given freedom (Num. 35:9-34, esp. verse 25)	*Through His death, all who were "dead" to God are given eternal freedom* (John 8:34-36, Rom. 6:22, 8:1-2, Eph. 2:1-10, etc.)

Christ's blood covers sins as a demonstration of mercy toward sinners. He does not merely hide our sins or forgive them in anticipation of some (yet) future action. Rather, He *properly removes them once for all*. While this was impossible under the Law of Moses, the Levitical sacrificial system foreshadowed it. Christ provided what was lacking in that system—the *uncorrupted blood of a perfect human specimen who was also a divine being*—and thus absolutely fulfilled the requirement *of* law in His own offering (Rom. 8:1-4).[49]

Christ was *tempted*, yet without sin (2:18; see Heb. 4:15). He faced what we face, but He did not succumb to that to which we have succumbed—the lies, delusion, and seduction of Satan's enticement to exalt and/or gratify ourselves. To be *like* His "brethren," He had to endure what they endure; to *intercede* for His brethren (as their Redeemer), He had to overcome that which had overcome them. Jesus was "tempted in what He has suffered," which means He bore sufferings as part of His temptation: He had the ability to forego these sufferings, but He accepted them instead (see Mat. 26:53). "This does not mean that he would not have had *power* to assist others if he had not gone through these sufferings, but that he is now qualified to sympathize with them [i.e., those who also suffer trials—MY WORDS] from the fact that he has endured like trials."[50]

---

[49] When someone asks, "Did Christ's blood fulfill the requirement of the Law of Moses, or did it inaugurate the law of Christ (i.e., the gospel)?" the answer must be *yes*. His blood accomplished both things at once: it brought closure to the one while establishing the other. It is incorrect to say that we are under God's covenant with Israel (or that we are under the Law of Moses) because we are under a new covenant that has superseded that one. However, it *is* accurate to say that Christ's blood provides a crucial link to the two covenants.

[50] Barnes, *Notes*, 74.

Section Two: Warnings against Apostasy (3:1—6:20)

First Warning against Apostasy (3:1–19)

"Therefore" (3:1) indicates that the writer is presenting the reader with a progressive, unfolding argument. While *we* have become "holy brethren, partakers of [or, sharers in] a heavenly calling" (see Rom. 8:28-30, 1 Cor. 1:9, and Eph. 3:6), Jesus has already become our forerunner as "the Apostle and High Priest of our confession." The writer asks readers to "consider" Jesus' supremacy.[51] There have been several apostles, but God speaks to us through His only begotten Son, the ideal Apostle (recall 1:1-2). We have many shepherds in the brotherhood, but only one Chief Shepherd (John 10:14, 1 Peter 5:4). The Jews had numerous high priests over the centuries, but Jesus is a greater High Priest than all of them. "Confession" here is directly linked to Jesus' high-priestly intercession (as in Heb. 4:14 and 10:23). It is the believer's personal profession of his conviction concerning Christ's redemptive work. One who confesses Christ (in this context) acknowledges His supremacy over all other lords or saviors—including Moses (Acts 7:35).[52]

---

51 "Consider" is an ideal word here. It is translated from a Greek word (*katanoesate*) meaning: to fix one's mind upon a thing (Robertson, *Word Pictures*, 353). Our English word is from Latin *con* (with) + *sideris* (stars or constellation), thus literally refers to a gazing in wonderment at the stars. "One who takes the time to behold the beauty and majesty of the night sky is literally *with the stars* in his thoughts and emotions and cannot fail to receive deep impressions of awe, wonder, and appreciation. It is with this very attitude that men are invited to consider Christ" (Coffman, *Commentary*, 66).

52 Jesus is also superior over Aaron and his high-priestly office, but the writer here concentrates only on Moses for now. In chapter 7, he will highlight Christ's superiority over the Aaronic or Levitical priesthood as well.

Christ's Superiority over Moses (3:2-6): While similarities do exist between the two men, Christ is far superior to Moses in all things (3:2-6). Moses was faithful to that which God had commission him (see Josh. 1:1-4) but he was not a perfect man: he had been tempted and *did* sin. Moses was faithful in the "house" of Israel (Num. 12:7) but Jesus was born the *King* of Israel (John 18:37). Moses built a "house" for God in the form of a physical tabernacle, but he was not the builder of Christ's church—a spiritual "house" that far exceeds the tabernacle. God is the Builder of Christ's church ("house") in the sense that it was constructed according to His plans and by His authority. But Christ is the One who *built* it, providing a spiritual sanctuary for those brought into it.[53]

Whatever Christ has spoken to us (recall 1:2, 2:3) is superior to whatever Moses spoke to Israel. Moses was a *servant* of God, but Christ is the *Son* of God; Moses served *in* God's "house," but Christ rules *over* it. Furthermore, Moses *belongs* to God's "house," but Christ *is the house*, in essence (3:6; see Col. 1:18, 1 Tim. 3:15, and 1 Peter 2:4-5). "We should not think of two houses, the Old Testament and the New Testament house; these are but one house that is composed of God's spiritual people."[54] *All* the faithful are now brought together in one "house" (see John 10:16 and Eph. 2:19-23).

A conditional premise does exist for our association with God, however: "*if* we hold fast our confidence...."[55] Christ promises us a place in God's "house," but only if "we" (believers) follow through with that to which

---

53 There is no contradiction here in saying that both God and Christ are the Builders of the same church. We see the same thing being done today, where a "builder" of a home or subdivision may have nothing to do with the physical construction of the house yet is credited with the power and authority *behind* that construction. In the same way, Moses "built" the tabernacle and Solomon "built" the temple, but neither man necessarily had anything to do with physically constructing these structures.

54 Lenski, *Interpretation*, 105.

55 In both places—Heb. 3:6 and Col. 1:23—the Calvinist dogma of "once saved, always saved" is clearly undermined. Salvation—like grace, forgiveness, and all of God's gifts to His saints—are conditioned upon sustained faithfulness. God's *love* is unconditional, but His love *by itself* does not save the human soul. We are saved *because* of His love for us but not *by* it.

we first committed (1 Tim. 6:12-14). The writer is thus warning those who are contemplating a defection from their confession of Christ as Lord. "These Hebrew Christians had confessed Jesus as their Apostle and High Priest. They do not begin to understand what Jesus is and means if they are tempted to give him up."[56]

The Exodus as an Allegory (3:7-11): "Therefore …" (3:7) again means we cannot separate what the writer is *about* to say from what he has *just* said. Even though Christ is the head of God's "house," no person will benefit from this who does not put *confidence* (obedient faith) in Christ until the very end. To support his argument, the writer draws upon the inspired writing of David (3:7-11, quoted from Psalm 95:7-11).[57] This quote refers to the first generation of Israel that God led out of Egyptian captivity and repeatedly refused to be faithful to Him. They "tested" God (i.e., tried His patience with their doubt and complaining) to the point where God refused to give them what He had originally promised them, since this promise was conditioned upon their faithfulness to Him (Num. 14:11, 22, 1 Cor. 10:1-5). To "harden your hearts" means to be insensitive and unresponsive toward God's commands. Because the Israelites disbelieved His ability to perform, the entire generation (save for two men) was condemned to die in the wilderness instead of entering the Promised Land (Canaan).

The spiritual application here is unavoidable: just as the Israelites lost their lives for unbelief, so a Christian can lose his soul for *his* unbelief (3:12).[58] Just as those Israelites were denied the Promised Land, so

---

56   Robertson, *Word Pictures*, 353.

57   David wrote this psalm with his own words, and according to his own personality, but the *substance* of what was said was provided by the Holy Spirit, as was the integrity and accuracy of its prophetic content. We will see this several more times in *Hebrews* where the writer credits the Holy Spirit as the source of the prophetic writings of David, Isaiah, Jeremiah, and other prophets (see 1 Peter 1:10-12). In this case, it is recommended that we read Psalm 95 in its entirety, recognizing that changes in wording are at least in part because the writer is quoting from the Septuagint (Greek translation of the Old Testament) rather than the Hebrew Bible. "All the Old Testament is to him a divine oracle, the voice of the Holy Spirit…" (Bruce, *Commentary*, 34).

58   "In a sense, Hebrews 3:12 may be called one of the nerve centers of the epistle" (Kistemaker, *NTC*, 99). This is because this warning reverberates throughout so much

an unbelieving Christian will be denied entrance into the kingdom of God. An "evil, unbelieving heart" does not have to commit acts of overt wickedness: he only needs to recant his profession of faith in Christ. If one turns away from Christ, there is no other savior to whom he can turn for salvation—not even Moses (since even Moses defers to Christ—see John 5:39-40, 45-47).

"Unbelief" does not mean what it may sound like to the unconverted mind. An atheist, for example, disbelieves in God: he does merely disbelieve what God said or revealed but he disbelieves in God's existence. (Atheists are quick to remind us of this distinction.) But the *Hebrews* writer speaks of an "unbelief" among Christians who, by virtue of their having *become* Christians, *do* believe that God exists and is the source of all divinely revealed doctrine. On the other hand—and this is the point being made by the writer—they do not *sincerely* believe, do not *actively* believe, and/or do not *fully* believe. Their "belief" is hindered, compromised, or limited in some way that undermines its effectiveness. They claim to be "believers" but do not respond, act, or live like true believers do.

Thus, Christians can believe in God, believe in Christ, believe in Christianity, and believe that the Bible is the word of God, yet still practice *unbelief* by not allowing these foundational beliefs to direct their lives, condition their hearts, and war against temptation and sin. Their beliefs are clinical, not life-changing; they believe in certain facts and details about God but not in His ability to perform. They claim to believe in God's power but do not avail themselves to that power. In effect, they claim to be submissive to God's will but are resisting that will all at once. In fact, all "unbelief" is resistance to God, and all resistance is a form of unbelief. Whenever God tells us to believe, do, or relinquish and we refuse to submit to this, we are resisting Him and therefore practice unbelief. It is *this* that the writer is talking about, not the refusal to believe *at all* or *in everything* about God.

---

of what else is said: God is a *Living God* who imparts life to those who believe in Him; but to those who manifest *unbelief*—especially those who *know better*—He lays a divine curse against them.

The urgent message here (in 3:13) is, in essence, "Respond to His voice *while there is still time to do so!*" We are instructed here to "encourage one another" to prevent such evil and unbelief from taking root in any Christian's heart (see Heb. 10:23-25)—while looking to ourselves as well (Gal. 6:1-2). The "deceitfulness of sin" will harden a person's heart (i.e., make him insensitive to God's grace) so that he will no longer listen to Christ's voice. On this passage, Coffman draws five important conclusions:[59]

1. It is possible for a Christian to "fall away" from God [as opposed to falling away from a mere religious or emotional experience—MY WORDS].
2. This falling away is inescapably due to an unbelieving heart.
3. Such a heart is not intelligent or wise but is decidedly evil.
4. God is not a mere moral force or influence in the world, but a Divine Personage ("the living and true God"—1 Thess. 1:9).
5. A Christian can avoid falling away by responding properly to what God (through Christ) speaks to us.

One who is in Christ will continue to be a partaker *of* Christ if he continues to "hold fast" his faith in Him "until the end" (3:14; see Col. 1:21-23 and Rev. 2:10). The writer then poses three rhetorical questions, based upon Psalm 95, to underscore his message (3:16-18):

1. Did Israel provoke God with their unbelief?—*yes, and they suffered disastrous consequences as a result.*
2. Was God angry with those people's unbelief?—*yes, to the point that He cursed them to die in the wilderness rather than enter the "rest" He had appointed for them.*
3. Did God swear that these disobedient people would not enter the Promised Land?—*yes, and [implied] you will not enter heaven, if you also practice unbelief.*

"So we see that they were not able to enter because of unbelief" (3:19). This is the essential point: unbelief is not only a sin but is ruinous to the

---

59 Coffman, *Commentary*, 78-79.

one who practices it. The Jewish Christians who were contemplating abandoning their faith in Christ were in danger of becoming *unbelievers*, even if they devoted themselves to Moses and Aaron. Likewise, Christians who turn away from Christ make themselves *unbelievers*, regardless of what or whom they turn to instead—even if it is done with good intentions or in the name of God.

The Danger of Forfeiting What Was Promised (4:1–13)

The Need for Faith (4:1-2): In this passage (4:1-13), the writer gives a second warning against apostasy [lit., turning away from the truth].[60] One's salvation needs to be pursued with "fear and trembling" (Phil. 2:12). First, it is a profound responsibility; second, the God *of* salvation is to be regarded with the utmost reverence. Thus, "let us fear" (4:1)—in a healthy, respectful, obedient manner. Reverence is a key theme throughout this epistle and needs to be just as emphasized today. God's promise of rest to the believer is conditioned upon that person's faithfulness to His covenant. In other words, the promise itself is not in question or prone to fail; rather, one's personal belief *in* that promise is the only variable.

As a historical case in point, ancient Israel had "good news" [lit., gospel] preached to them, but they did not benefit from it (4:2). This was not because the good news was unable to help them, but because they did not put faith *in* it. "They" refers to the Israelites who had come out of Egypt, passed through the Red Sea, and observed many signs and wonders. God had given them every reason to believe in His ability to perform, yet they chronically persisted in unbelief. This culminated in their refusal to believe that God could bring them into the Promised

---

60   I discuss at length what "apostasy" is, what departure from the truth looks like, and why people turn away from the truth in my book, *The New Testament Pattern: God's Plan for Christians and Their Churches* (Spiritbuilding Publishers, 2023); go to www.spiritbuilding.com/chad.

Land (4:3-5). Likewise, we (Christians) have had the gospel preached to us, and we have believed it; but if we do not continue *in* belief, then this good news will be of no benefit to us. In that case, the gospel which was meant to save us will instead condemn us (Rom. 11:22).

God's "Rest" for Believers (4:3-11): The writer ties God's "rest" (from His work of the Creation—Gen. 2:1-3) with the "rest" He promises to Christians (4:3-11). God could only "rest" from this work because He finished it.[61] However, our work (discipleship to Christ) remains unfinished, so we cannot yet "rest" from it. The writer here touches on a profound point: the "rest" that follows a completed work is itself a part *of* that work. The two actions—working and resting—go together: one's work anticipates a "rest" from it, and one's "rest" implies that the work which he performed is in fact finished.[62] Once we complete our ministry to Christ on earth, we will enter God's rest that He now enjoys having completed *His* work of Creation.

However, if one fails to complete his work (due to his unbelief), he forfeits the rest God had promised him. God has provided the *time* for responding to this "good news": it is "today"—and God promises no one a tomorrow (4:6-7; see James 4:13-17). This is true for the backsliding Christian as it is for one who remains outside of Christ. In a parallel thought, God promised Israel rest from their enemies in Canaan as long as they remained faithful to Him (4:8; see Deut. 12:10). Yet, Joshua never gave to Israel the kind of rest that Christ offers us: theirs was physical (an inheritance of land); ours is spiritual (an eternal home in God's kingdom). To enjoy this spiritual rest, one must respond *now*

---

61   This is a specific reference to a specific act: the Creation. In other words, because He rested from *that* work (since it has been completed) does not mean He rests from *all* work (that remains ongoing), or that He does not have *any* work (an idea of which is the underpinning of Deism). For a detailed explanation of this, see McClister, "Excursus: The Sabbath Rest," *Commentary*, 135-150.

62   We cannot help but think of Christ, who fully carried out all the work which God had given Him and thus had every right to enter rest from His earthly ministry (John 17:4-5, 19:30). Not only does this point undermine modern Premillennialism (which claims that Christ must return to earth for another 1,000 years of work) but it inarguably proves that Christ's work was indeed "once for all," as the writer later declares (Heb. 10:10, etc.).

("today") while the window of opportunity still exists; otherwise, he may forfeit this opportunity altogether.[63]

A "Sabbath rest" (4:9) indicates the *kind* of rest of which the writer speaks.[64] God imposed a Sabbath rest upon Israel in honor of His own rest from the work of Creation (Exod. 20:8-11). This rest (day) was observed as the seventh day of every week, as the final part of the entire cycle of a seven-day period. (Note: the "rest" was *part* of the full week, not separate from it.) In the spiritual context, a "Sabbath rest" indicates the completion of *all* the believer's earthly work since he will have entered God's "rest" forever (4:10). Unlike what Israel faced, there will be no *new* cycle (a new week) beginning after this, since one's life here on earth will then be finished forever. The "work(s)" from which believers will rest includes the following:

❏ Endurance of physical life in general.
❏ Breathing, drinking, eating; daily sustenance for the human body.
❏ The need for (and securing of) shelter, clothing, heat, protection, etc.
❏ Dealing with waste(s) of the human body and of this world.
❏ Physical labor to be done—if not directly for the above needs, then for money or income to purchase these things.
❏ Dealing with human imperfections—one's own and those of everyone else.
❏ Responsibility for oneself—physical needs, hygiene, stewardship of one's possessions and resources, behavior, reputation, godliness, etc.
❏ Responsibility for others—spouse, children, relatives, friends, brethren, "neighbors" in general (including one's community, government, etc.).

---

63 This means that one must *act in obedience to the command of God*. This plea is not limited to those who have yet to become Christians; in the present case (as in the case of 2 Cor. 6:1-2) it applies to those who have already believed, but who are in danger of being unbelieving. God gives His grace freely to those who so respond, but His grace is "in vain" to those who turn away from Him toward anything else.

64 Here, the Greek word is *sabbatismos*, lit., "a Sabbath-keeping" or Sabbath observance; it is the only time this word is used in the NT (McClister, *Commentary*, 169).

- Attention to the word of God—its demands and implications, and the necessary changes and adaptations of our lives to accommodate these.
- Dealing with sin—whatever this involves, including the struggle to overcome it.
- Endurance of the sinful world (i.e., living under a curse—Gen. 3:17-19).
- Evangelism—our responsibility to rightly represent and share the gospel.

None of these earthly activities will carry over into the afterlife. In heaven, the believer will enjoy a "Sabbath rest" from all these conditions, functions, impositions, and curses; he will no longer experience hunger, thirst, weariness, sorrow, pain, etc. (Rev. 7:16-17). This does not mean there will be no work for us in the hereafter—this is simply not addressed here—but that rest from earthly life will be perpetual and irreversible.

"Therefore let us be diligent to enter that rest..." (4:11). "Diligence" involves earnest endeavor, applied effort, and a sense of urgency (as in Rom. 12:10-11 and 2 Peter 1:5). The believer is admonished to exert himself productively in anticipation of his "rest" with the Lord. Entrance into the eternal kingdom is not easy (Acts 14:22), and we must "Strive to enter" it (Luke 13:24). Even so, "rest" is entirely within the reach of anyone in Christ who practices his faith in Him. One must do well to avoid the faithlessness and disobedience of Israel (see 1 Cor. 10:1-12).

The Discerning Word of God (4:12-13): Having just discussed being *diligent* (unlike Israel) rather than *disobedient* (like Israel), the writer now warns his readers: *do not think God is unaware of the true disposition of your heart* (4:12-13). His "word" is otherworldly sharp: it divides what cannot be humanly divided. It also cuts both ways, just like a Roman "two-edged sword"—meaning, it can both defend *or* destroy a human soul. God sees every object, person, and soul; nothing escapes His notice, not even what is (to us) invisible, indiscernible, and imperceptible.

The "word" does not define exactly what the human "soul" or "spirit" is but can *divide* (or make a distinction between) the two.[65] One's "soul" likely refers to his non-tangible existence—the invisible essence of his life—whereas his "spirit" refers to his thoughts, conscience, and rational mind (1 Thess. 5:23).[66] Where the actual division is between these two invisible aspects of one's being is known only by God's Spirit, not human comprehension. The natural sense of "joints and marrow" is used figuratively "to denote the inmost essence of man's spiritual nature,"[67] that is, in another reference to human life invisible to the human eye (and even the human heart) but fully revealed to God. "The Word of God is the only power that can penetrate so deeply and expose so completely the inwardness of our being."[68]

The "word of God" here is not the literal Bible since words on pages are neither living nor active. Rather, it refers to the authority and ability of God's Holy Spirit—the One who has revealed what Scripture has recorded. His "word"—the commandments, their power, and their convicting and transforming effect—is elsewhere called "the sword of the Spirit" (Eph. 6:17), which parallels the present passage. The writer of *Hebrews* never refers to Jesus as "the word of God" but instead as "the Son of God" (4:14).

Granted, it is difficult for us to separate the work of Christ from the work of the Spirit (cf. Rom. 8:26-27 and 1 Tim. 2:4-5); granted also, Jesus is called the "Word" elsewhere in Scripture (John 1:1, Rev. 19:13). But in

---

65 "That the word of God probes the inmost recesses of our spiritual being and brings the subconscious motives to light is what is meant; we may compare Paul's language about the coming day when the Lord 'will both bring to light the hidden things of darkness, and make manifest the counsels of the hearts (1 Cor. 4:5)" (Bruce, *Commentary*, 82). See also Rom. 2:16, where Paul talks about the "secrets of men" being judged through Christ.

66 "Spirit" is from *pneuma*, which can also be translated "soul," "wind," or "breath." In 4:12 (as in 1 Thess. 5:23), "spirit" is from *pneuma*, whereas "soul" is from *psyche*. In James 2:26, however, translators use the word "spirit" when it is elsewhere rendered "soul." This makes our understanding of these terms more difficult, but the definition provided in the comments above indicate their most typical usage in Scripture.

67 Milligan, *Commentary*, 139.

68 Lenski, *Interpretation*, 143.

the present context, "word of God" refers to the dynamic and convicting *power* and *omniscience* of God's Spirit (as in John 16:8-11, which speaks of the work of the Spirit among men; see also 1 Peter 1:23-25). The Holy Spirit speaks the "word of God" to people, and whatever He says and does is full of life and activity (John 6:63). It is the Spirit that both reveals and convicts the human heart, just as He has revealed God's will to us through the Scriptures. The Bible is the written record of *what* the Spirit does but not *how* He does it.[69]

This passage (4:12-13) in some respect alludes to the Levitical priests' responsibilities toward the animals brought by Israelites to be sacrificed to God (Lev. 22:17-25). The priests had a legal responsibility to ensure that all such animals were fit for sacrifice, having no defect or blemish. In a comparable way, as we approach the throne of God in fellowship, in communion, and with our petitions, Christ (through the agency of the Holy Spirit) scrutinizes each of us intimately and penetratingly. As our High Priest, He has the legal responsibility to do this, as He cannot allow any person to approach God apart from His approval (John 14:6, in principle).

Yet, while His examination of us is parallel to that of the Levitical priests, it is also superior to it in every way. The ancient priests could make mistakes or misdiagnoses; they could be swayed by their feelings for the one bringing the offering to be more lenient on his animal's worthiness; they could be corrupt (see Mal. 1:6-9); or the animal could have some internal problem (sickness or disease) that could not be detected by human examination. Christ, however, is not subject to all such problems or limitations. Nothing escapes His detection; every soul is "laid bare" before Him; He sees *everything*, even far beyond all human comprehension.

---

69 I recommend my book, *The Holy Spirit of God: A Biblical Perspective* (Waynesville, OH: Spiritbuilding Publishers, 2010) for a fuller explanation of this passage; go to www.spiritbuilding.com/chad.

Christ as Our High Priest
(4:14—5:10)

Approaching the Throne of Grace (4:14-16): The believer does not have to fear the scrutiny of an all-seeing God on his own since Jesus—"a great high priest"—advocates and mediates for him (4:14-16). Instead of merely passing through a veil into the innermost sanctuary of the temple, as a Levitical high priest would have done, Jesus came before the actual Presence of God. Notice the writer here uses "Jesus" rather than "Christ": Jesus who had endured life on this earth as one of us now sits on His throne at the right hand of God as *Christ the Son of God* (Acts 2:33, Heb. 8:1).

In this capacity, He serves as both *King* and *High Priest* of God's kingdom. No high priest of Israel ever sat on a throne; no king of Israel ever ministered as a high priest. Priests mediate, kings rule; priests work standing up (at the altar), kings work sitting down (upon a throne). The fact that our High Priest reigns on a throne as a great King indicates the merging of two offices into one (Zech. 6:11-13).

Christians are to approach Christ's "throne of grace" with *confidence*, which can only be gained if we "hold fast [or, cling tightly to] our confession." This confession (here) alludes to our original commitment to Christ (1 Tim. 6:12). The substance of *His* confession—His innocence, worthiness, and perfect obedience—gives life and meaning to *our* confession. And, since He knows what it is like to be human and endure the temptations and struggles of this life, He serves as the ideal intercessor between us and God (1 Tim. 2:4).[70] As our High Priest, He does not merely act in an official capacity, carrying out the rites and

---

70 "The crucial difference between us and Jesus, however, is that not once did he ever give in to temptation. He never allowed temptation to turn into sin. In case it might be argued that this could only make Jesus *less* sympathetic to others ('how could he be sympathetic to the plight of sinners if he never sinned?'), it should be noted that it takes much more strength of character and will, and purity of heart, to resist temptation and remain faithful than it does to give in to temptation and sin. Enduring is always harder than surrendering" (McClister, *Commentary*, 180).

functions expected of one in such a position, but is *personally aware* of our struggles and can *identify* with "our weaknesses" (i.e., of being human). In fact, we cannot even identify with what He endured here in the same way He can identify with us. Thus, instead of *withdrawing* from Christ's "throne of grace" in unbelief, fear, or indifference, Christians are admonished to *draw near* to Him (4:16; see James 4:8). No one else possesses His credentials; no one else can give what He offers (John 6:67-68).

In our presentation before Christ (through prayer), we "receive mercy" and "find grace" (4:16). "Mercy" or compassion is the withholding of what is deserved (as punishment); "grace" is whatever is undeserved or unearned (as a gift). But mercy is more than the mere withholding of something bad; it is also the offering of what is *needed* for comfort or consolation—whatever relieves one's present difficulty or distress (like what the good Samaritan offered in Luke 10:30-37). Christ's "throne of grace" symbolizes His all-sufficient atonement (or high-priestly work) and all-sufficient authority (or kingly work): the first work *makes* us worthy; the second *pronounces* us worthy. When we stand before the throne of judgment (2 Cor. 5:10), those who have drawn near to the throne of grace will have nothing to fear.[71]

A Comparison of the Priesthoods (5:1-10): The earthly high priests of the Levitical order—namely, Aaron and his sons—were adequate for their time but had insurmountable limitations. They were "taken from among men" (5:1)—i.e., they could act on behalf of men but could not overcome their own human deficiencies. Even so, the high priests stood (in a sense) between God and men. To God, they offered gifts

---

71 "Precisely because it is a throne of grace and not a judgment seat, this is why it can be approached with confidence (*parresia*). *Parresia* (from *pan* + *resia* = full story) in ancient Greece denoted the right of a full citizen to speak his mind on any subject in the town assembly—a right that the slave did not have. In the Epistle it stands for freedom to approach God on the basis of the blood of Jesus (10:19). Before God's throne Christians need not have fears and inhibitions" (Lightfoot, *Jesus Christ Today*, 101). Our word "confidence" is appropriate as well: "con-" (with) + "fide" (faith); thus, the state of having faith (in something).

and sacrifices[72]; to men, they offered intercession to God and pardon for men's offenses. The priests dealt with (spiritually) "ignorant and misguided" people (5:2), yet they were constantly aware of their own imperfections since they had to make sacrifices for their own sins before ministering to the needs of others (Lev. 16:6).[73]

As important as his role was, Aaron (or his successors) never declared himself a high priest apart from being "called by God" (5:4). This means that God ordained the priesthood (through the Law of Moses), not men.[74] Had God not set Aaron (and his posterity) aside *for* the priesthood, he could not have legitimately served in this capacity. This is significant because it shows his priesthood as being *subservient* to the Law rather than transcendent of it (as Jesus' is). This will be discussed further shortly.

"So also Christ did not glorify Himself" (5:5): as Aaron did not appoint himself a high priest, neither did Christ appoint Himself a high priest. God the Father conferred upon Aaron the high priesthood; He also conferred upon Christ *His* high priesthood. Aaron's appointment was through the Law; Christ's was through a divine oath (5:5-6; see Heb. 7:20-21). Just as God declared Christ as King (Acts 2:33), by virtue of Him being the Son of God, so He declared Christ to be "a priest forever." Both facts are confirmed by prophecies (Psalm 2:7 and 110:4). In other words, as God appointed Aaron as high priest of a temporary order, He also appointed Christ as a high priest of an eternal order.

---

72 Since the writer here is speaking of duties exclusive to the high priest, we are made to think of the offerings of atonement and consecration offered on the Day of Atonement (Lev. 16). These included bloody offerings and non-bloody gifts.

73 Milligan (*Commentary*, 151) rightly notes that the Day of Atonement was not the only occasion on which the high priest had to acknowledge his own sins but was simply the most notable occasion.

74 This is graphically demonstrated in the case of Korah's rebellion (Num. 16), in which Korah sought to become a priest on par with Aaron, even though he was not of the family of Levi which God had selected for this purpose. God's judgment against Korah (and company) underscores the Law's appointment of its high priests.

"In the days of His flesh" (5:7)—a reference to when Jesus was here upon this earth as a Man (John 1:14; see 2 Cor. 5:16). The writer here alludes to Jesus' anguished prayer in the garden of Gethsemane, just prior to His arrest (Mat. 26:36-46). While it may appear that Jesus prayed *not to die*, the real essence of His prayer is that *His Father's will be done*, regardless of the cost.[75] "Here is seen God's method of answering prayers in some instances, in which he sends not a lighter burden but a stronger heart to bear it."[76] This surrender to the Father's will is the "piety" (i.e., reverence, godly fear, or religious devotion) to which the writer refers. Thus, Jesus' work as our High Priest began on earth *in anticipation* of it being fully realized in heaven. He was born to reign as a King (Mat. 2:2, John 18:37) but also to minister as a priest: the voluntary offering of Himself proved this (Heb. 7:27).

While Jesus was already worthy of the throne of David *and* the kingdom of God by virtue of His divine Sonship, He still needed to prove His *personal* worthiness through obedience to His Father (5:8). However, He did not "learn" obedience like we do—through trial and error; through resistance (first) then submission (ultimately). From His youth, Jesus *knew* what obedience was, then *practiced* it, even *experienced* it in full measure in His sacrificial death (Phil. 2:8). It was not that He had to be taught *how* to obey; rather, He had to "learn" what it *felt like* to obey even through immense suffering. Through perfect obedience, He became "the source [or, author] of eternal salvation" (5:9) for all those who also are striving to be obedient to God—not with Jesus' same flawlessness but sharing His attitude of submission (John 8:29, Rom. 6:17-18, and 1 Peter 2:21-22).

In proving Himself worthy for the office, Jesus was declared (or, designated; ordained) by God "as a high priest forever according to the

---

75 Compare Jesus' (and the Father's) words in John 12:26-27 and 18:11. Jesus knew that he would have to drink the "cup," yet He (in His humanity) recoiled from the horror of it—not only the act of crucifixion itself but what He (as a sin offering) would have to bear during that crucifixion.

76 Coffman, *Commentary*, 109.

order of Melchizedek"[77] (5:10), a reference to the king-priest of Salem whom Abraham encountered after his battle with the kings of the east (Gen. 14). Melchizedek served prophetically as a type of the future Messiah in several aspects (which will be discussed in chapter 7). Jesus' priesthood is based upon the dual office (the "order") of Melchizedek, even while fulfilling the symbolic forms prefigured in the Levitical priesthood. Even so, as significant as the roles of Melchizedek and the Aaronic priesthood were, no man could secure "eternal salvation" for *anyone*—including himself—except for Jesus Christ.

Second Warning against Apostasy (5:11—6:20)

The Danger of Dullness of Hearing: The *Hebrews* writer has thus far expounded upon Christ's superiority to angels, humankind, Moses, and Aaron. Yet all this is lost upon those whose senses are dulled with mediocre (spiritual) education and whose hearts are laced with doubt (5:11). The original recipients of this letter had far too much time and opportunity to be wavering between two beliefs—i.e., Moses and Christ. They should have been much more grounded than they were; they ought to have been *defending* and *imitating* Christ rather than contemplating their abandonment of Him.

Yet distraction, disinterest, fear, lack of diligence, and inadequate preparation on their part had left them soft, unfocused, and undisciplined—thus, they were gullible, weak, and seeking the path of least resistance. The writer wants to say much more about this Melchizedek and how Christ's office is patterned after his (and he will shortly), but he does not want to waste his time doing so to those who

---

[77] "The word *forever*...means here, as in many other passages of Scripture, *while time endures*. As the duration of the Aaronic priesthood was coextensive with the Jewish age..., so also is the duration of Christ's priesthood to be coextensive with the Christian age. But at the close of the Christian dispensation, when he shall have delivered up the Kingdom to the Father...he will doubtless cease to act as a Priest; for then the object of his priesthood, as well as of his mediatorial reign, will have been accomplished" (Milligan, *Commentary*, 155, emphases are his).

will not appreciate this instruction.

Likewise, every church today has those who are stuck on "elementary principles," who never seem to get past the basics (5:12-13). Deliberate immaturity—through lack of desire, effort, and growth—is never acceptable to God. Those who have been Christians long enough to take on the responsibilities of teachers, but remain forever students or even bystanders, will never learn to appreciate Christ's work, priesthood, or salvation. ("Teachers" here does not necessarily mean literal Bible class teachers but refers to those who actively promote the gospel's teaching in whatever way is needed and appropriate; see 2 Tim. 2:2.) Like an adult who must be nourished again as though a young child, so is the backward and dysfunctional condition of one who, despite all the advantages provided for him, reverts to an infantile spiritual life (1 Cor. 13:11). Instead of moving forward, he is stuck on "elementary principles."

"But solid food is for the mature" (5:14)—this refers to what a person can *swallow*: the "infant" believer, only milk; the mature believer, meat and solid food (1 Cor. 3:1-2). The mature Christian has his senses "trained to discern good and evil," that is, to effectively discriminate or judge between what is to be believed (or useful) and what is not (or useless). Such training, and the discernment that follows, is no accident; it does not happen naturally over time; it is not to be assumed (Eph. 4:14, Col. 2:8). The writer's original reading audience, in failing to appreciate the united offices of Christ's kingship and priesthood, are not showing mature discernment. "Spiritual growth is not an academic exercise but is protection against unfaithfulness."[78]

There is nothing wrong with elementary teachings of Christ (6:1-3). Every believer must begin with these and learn them well. Yet, *having* learned such teachings, one is expected to grow beyond them.[79]

---

78   McClister, *Commentary*, 204.
79   Bruce points out that the items listed among the elementary teachings are as much Jewish as they are Christian. These doctrines may have carried over from teachings from the Essene and Qumran communities—radically conservative Jews—

Instead of repeating the same primary concepts, digressing into endless discussions on petty religious doctrines, or constantly being re-taught "the issues," Christians are to "press on to maturity [or, perfection; completeness]" and *move forward* in their faith (Phil. 3:14). Once we have been grounded in the foundational teachings (like repentance, faith toward God, baptism, etc.), we are expected to advance beyond these.[80] This does not mean we can never re-visit subjects we have once learned; it means we should not permanently *camp* on these, and even in revisiting them we should do so with greater understanding. A foundation only needs to be laid once; once it is laid, it can be strengthened, but it remains what it is. There is much more to a structure than just its foundation.

The Peril of Unbelief (6:4-8): This next passage (6:4-8) is one of the most unsettling of this entire epistle. Perhaps preachers and teachers have watered down these words with assurances that, no matter how many times a Christian "falls away," he can always come back. While in some cases this may be true (depending upon how one defines "falls away"), in other cases this may *not* be true. Lenski, for one, writes on this passage:

> Both those who were never converted and those who have been converted may fall into a state in which they make repentance impossible. They may already in this life reach a state that is similar to that of the damned in hell, yea, a state that is similar to

---

rather than mainstream Judaism. Later, they may have been given prominence in the Christian church, even more so than in the Jewish synagogue (Bruce, *Commentary*, xxix, 112).

80 Obviously, subjects like "washings" (likely a reference to baptisms or purification rites beyond what was required to become a Christian), "laying on of [the apostles'] hands" (likely, the transmission of miraculous gifts in general), the future resurrection of the saints, and "eternal judgment" were challenging believers in the first century as they continue to challenge people today. These subjects deserve intelligent and biblical responses, to be sure. On the other hand, the Scriptures offer limited information on them and will never satisfy everyone's questions. The point here seems to be this: learn what you can from the Scriptures, revisiting these teachings as needed, but do not be immobilized by teachings that, in the end, do not change the message of salvation or our moral responsibility to God.

that of the devils, for whom there is no repentance, no pardon. Although this is terrible beyond words, it is, nevertheless, true. Repentance may be lost and found again; it may also become impossible exactly as here stated. God alone knows when the latter occurs; we can have only fears.[81]

While it does seem clear that this passage (6:4-6) deals with those who have completely abandoned the faith (i.e., apostatized), it should be said that one who, through neglect, indifference, or unbelief, even toys with doing so puts his soul in terrible jeopardy.[82] If any passage in the NT confirms the possibility of a Christian losing his soul, this is it. The language is clear and unmistakable; this is a person who:

- was once "enlightened."
- had "tasted of the heavenly gift"—that is, of divine grace (Rom. 3:23-24).
- had been made a "partaker of the Holy Spirit"—having been sealed and anointed by Him (2 Cor. 1:21-22).
- had "tasted of the good word of God and the powers of the age to come"—i.e., had benefited already from God's blessings and promises, as described in His word.

This does not describe a person who *thought* he was a Christian yet was mistaken. It describes a person who had indeed *become* a child of God, then turned his back on such sonship and privilege. Upon his having "fallen away," his restoration is "impossible"; in this case, he cannot be renewed merely with "repentance."[83] If a person does not respond to the

---

81 Lenski, *Interpretation*, 180.

82 "He is not speaking of mere backsliding, of the ordinary shortcomings and failures that go with human weakness. Falling short is not the same as falling away. It is one thing to yield to sin contrary to the new life in Christ, it is another thing to abandon that new life altogether" (Lightfoot, *Jesus Christ Today*, 126).

83 "[T]he context here shows plainly that the wilful [*sic*] sin which he has in mind is deliberate apostasy. People who commit this sin, he says, cannot be brought back to repentance; by renouncing Christ they put themselves in the position of those who, deliberately refusing His claim to be the Son of God, had Him crucified and exposed to public shame" (Bruce, *Commentary*, 124).

gospel after having already received it, nothing else can be done for him. "When the cord of life and love that binds the true believer to Christ, has been once completely severed, the parties so separated can never again be reunited. The case of the apostate is as hopeless as that of Satan himself."[84] His heart is so callous that not even the greatest events in all history and the universe—namely, that God "in the flesh" died for his sins and then rose from the dead—will affect him. No wonder Peter is so graphic (2 Peter 2:20-22), stating that that man's "last state" is worse than before he ever became a believer. He is now doubly condemned: not only is he overcome with sin, but he has forfeited the opportunity to escape his demise.

The warning here is most serious: one who walks away from Christ, after having welcomed His salvation, is identified with those who nailed Him to His cross (6:6). (This latter "crucify" is obviously figurative yet carries the same weight of guilt as the real thing.)[85] The difference here is that those who crucified Jesus did so largely in ignorance (see Luke 23:34 and 1 Cor. 2:6-8). This person, however, is not acting in ignorance but in sheer defiance, treason, and unbelief, being wholly unconcerned for the price that was paid for his forgiveness (2 Peter 1:9). Having walked away from the only source of divine forgiveness that exists, he abandons any hope for receiving forgiveness in this life or the life to come.
"For the ground that drinks the rain" (6:7)—a reference to the heart that gladly receives the kindness, blessings, and patience of God and bears much fruit (Rom. 7:4, Col. 1:9-10, etc.). This person flourishes in the Lord since he has responded favorably to His incentives. However, the person who "drinks" God's good gifts yet produces nothing of any value—because of his negligence, indifference, laziness, or unbelief—brings upon himself a curse (6:8).[86] In a similar analogy, Jesus declared

---

84 Milligan, *Commentary*, 178.

85 The "to themselves" phrase seems challenging: how does one crucify Jesus *to himself*? The answer appears to be: while he does not carry out a literal reenactment of the Lord's actual crucifixion, *in his own heart* he treats Jesus as if a guilty criminal, having no personal appreciation for His sacrifice, and therefore regards Him as expendable—Someone he can safely walk away from in pursuit of something else. In effect, Jesus is dead to him; he has crucified Him (put Him to death in his heart).

86 A suitable comparison can be found in Isa. 5:1-7, where God gave Israel every

that "branches" (believers) who "bear fruit" find favor with God; those who do not are "thrown away ... and cast ... into the fire" (John 15:1-6).

All this says something significant about the power of persuasion that the darkness has over believers, when they allow it to have controlling influence over their heart. Considering this wicked influence, it is important to recognize—more than ever—the value of keeping one's faith in God healthy, nurtured, and growing. It also indicates that one's faith is under constant attack, and that attending worship services and being involved with church functions are not enough by themselves to protect us. The same "diligence" with which we are to supply our faith (2 Peter 1:5-7) is also to be used in keeping our hope alive "until the end" (see 6:11).

Recollections of Former Deeds and Enthusiasm (6:9-12): Despite the strong language of the last several verses, the writer tones down his message now (6:9), as if to say, "While you are in danger, not all is lost *yet*." "[W]e are convinced of better things concerning you"—i.e., you are capable of improvement, and this is what is expected. Such language manifests an experienced approach to motivating people to do well, despite how poorly they might be performing presently. In other words, this writer is no amateur at encouraging weak brethren. Sadly, it appears he has had to do this often.

A critical rush to judgment would have disregarded all the good that had been accomplished and focused only on the negative situation. Yet God is not unjust (or, unrighteous) so as to overlook all that has been done in His honor (6:10). The writer's implied question to his readers is: will *you* be unjust by turning your back upon all *He* has done for *you*? Diligence of faith is required on their part; without such diligence, believers become "sluggish"—lazy, lethargic, dull of thinking, and unmotivated.

---

reason to succeed but they turned their backs on Him and gave Him only worthless fruit. See also Luke 13:6-9, where Jesus' parable makes it clear that God gives His gifts with the expectation that something good in return will be produced in us.

On the other hand, if they remain steadfast in hope, they will follow in the footsteps of those who have *already inherited* the promises (6:11-12). Hope provides motivation and inspiration to press forward; faith provides the necessary confidence in the One who gives *life* to hope. The "each one of you" phrase (6:11) indicates that faith is not (here) a collective action but an individual one. There is no allowance for some to ride the coattails of others; each person must be diligent in his own faith.

The Steadfast Anchor of God's Promise (6:13-20): While much has been said about Abraham's faithfulness to God (in Scripture and commentaries), here the writer emphasizes God's faithfulness to Abraham (6:13). It is true that Abraham "patiently waited" *twenty-five years* for his "hope" (Isaac, the son of promise) to be realized (6:14-15). Yet, it was God who made this hope possible against all human effort and ability (Rom. 4:16-22). In His promise to Abraham, God "swore by Himself": He invoked His own holy Name as a guarantee of that promise. This means that if God had *failed* to keep His promise, He would have violated His own divine nature.[87]

Since this is an impossible thing to do—for God to lie (Titus 1:2), be unfaithful, or deny Himself (2 Tim. 2:13)—He provides absolute assurance to the one to whom the promise is made. An "oath" is not just a spoken promise but carries with it the binding force of the thing or authority by which it is sworn. Men swear by an authority greater than themselves, but God must swear by His own Name since there is no greater name or authority. Thus, we see "two unchangeable things": first, God's unalterable divine nature; second, His oath (promise) which is supported by that divine nature (6:16-18).

---

87 It goes further than this. In Gen. 15:8-21, when Abraham was instructed to divide the animals in half and lay them on the ground, God made a binding covenant with him there. As God "walked" between the animals (as indicated by the "flaming torch"), He essentially said to Abraham: "If I fail to uphold My covenant with you, then you have the right to make Me like these animals—you have the right to *put Me to death*" (see Jer. 34:18-20). As it was, God voluntarily gave His own life (through His Son) to secure the *everlasting covenant* which guarantees the salvation of men's souls, as brought about through His promise to Abraham (Gal. 3:15-16).

Just as Abraham hoped in a God who cannot lie, fail, or be bound by human limitations, so Christians are to hope in this same God. Jesus Christ is the realization of that hope: in Him we have "taken refuge" (6:18).[88] We can take "strong encouragement" in who Christ is, what He has accomplished, and how He can help us. "This hope we have as an anchor of the soul" (6:19-20)—an excellent metaphor: the believer has *stability* and a *connection* to something immovable despite the storms of life, trials of faith, etc., just like a ship that is held fast on the water's surface despite the tempest.

But the Hebrew Christians, not much a seafaring people, would more readily identify with One who enters "within the veil," that is, as a high priest (see Lev. 16:11-14). Thus, our hope is securely embedded in the One who has entered within the *heavenly* veil already, "as a forerunner for us." For now, just as the anchor on the bottom of the ocean is invisible to the sailor, so Christ in heaven is (so far) invisible to the believer—but this will not always be the case.

It is important to note that Aaron, despite his role as a Levitical high priest, has never been identified as a "forerunner" for us. Christ, however, is so identified (6:20). He has done things for us that Aaron could never do; He has gone places (so to speak) for us that Aaron could never have gone; and He intercedes for us in ways that far supersede however Aaron interceded for the nation of Israel. Aaron's role was limited in ability, understanding, and duration; Christ's role as our eternal High Priest has no such limitations.

Having admonished his readers for their lax attention, the writer will resume where he left off in speaking of Melchizedek, and especially of the high priesthood of Christ (in chapter 7).

---

88 The allusion here is to the cities of refuge, where one guilty of involuntary manslaughter was able to seek protection from the "avenger of blood" (Num. 35). In that scenario, he had to remain in a city of refuge until the death of the high priest. Likewise, the Christian seeks refuge in Christ from the Avenger of our souls—for our having been responsible for the death of His Son—but since our High Priest never dies, we are forever safe in Him.

SECTION THREE:
A NEW PRIESTHOOD AND COVENANT (7:1—10:18)

The New Priesthood Not Based on Law (7:1–22)

We do not know anything about Melchizedek than what is written in Gen. 14:18-20 and here (7:1-3). Not everyone believes that he was even a real, historical person. Some differing views are stated here for perspective:[89]

- Theodot (200 BC), of the sect of the Melchizedekites, made him to be even superior to the Messiah, making Jesus a mere copy of *him*.
- Rabbi Ismael (ca. 135 BC) thought him to be Shem, Noah's son (as did Martin Luther and others).
- Philo (a contemporary of Christ) thought him to be the human soul personified, "divine reason functioning in a priestly way."
- Origen (AD 2nd c.) thought him to be an angel.
- Hierakas (AD 3rd c.) thought him to be the Holy Spirit in the flesh.
- Others have argued that he *was* Christ, in an "in the flesh" pre-appearance or theophany [lit., showing of God].

Despite such conjectures, Scripture presents Melchizedek as a real, flesh-and-blood, historical person, in the same context as Abraham and King Chedorlaomer (whom Abraham fought against and defeated). This is what we know of him:

- He was a king of Salem, likely the city-state of what was later known as Jerusalem.
- He was a priest of Most High God [Heb., *El Elyon*, an expression only used of Jehovah] though he lived some 500 years before the

---
[89] Lenski, *Interpretation*, 207.

- Levitical priesthood.
- He met Abraham (then, still "Abram") after his victory in battle and blessed him.
- He received from Abraham "a tenth part of all the spoils"[90] gained through his victory over the kings of the east.
- His name means "king of righteousness" [Heb., *melchi* = "(my) king"; *zedek* = righteousness].
- Since Salem (his domain) means "peace," he was also known as "king of peace."
- He was "without father, without mother, without genealogy"—while some take this literally, it is meant figuratively, in the context of what one would normally expect of a great priest-king. In other words, he descended from no chosen ancestry or dynasty (like Aaron did, being a descendent of Levi). Thus, neither his priesthood *nor* his kingship was based upon human lineage.
- He had "neither beginning of days nor end of life"—again, figuratively-speaking, his age is not recorded, nor his birth or death; compare this to the patriarchs in *Genesis*. It was *as though* he simply appeared out of nowhere, received tithes from Abraham, and then retreated into obscurity, beyond the record of human history.
- He was "made like the Son of God"—not *being* the Son, but his office foreshadows that *of* the Son; in a sense, he was a *type* of "Son of God" yet to come.
- He "remains a priest perpetually"—that is, since there is no record of his beginning or end, his presence in history continues without closure, permanently sustained.
- To summarize, he is neither an ordinary man nor a divine figure; he is mysterious, unknown, unprecedented, and unexpected.

Abraham was a great man, to be sure, but even he paid tithes to Melchizedek (7:4). Abraham was great because of his faith and covenant relationship with God, but Melchizedek was great because of his position as a king *and* a high priest of God. A "tenth" [lit., tithe] represents an honorable representation of one's income or gain.

---

90 Lit., a tithe; "a tenth of the top of the heap" of the spoils—i.e., the best part (Kistemaker, *NTC*, 187).

Centuries later, Levites were to receive a tenth of every Israelite's income per the Law of Moses; a tenth of the Levite's own income was given to the priests themselves (7:5; see Num. 18:21, 24-26).

But Levites were descendants of Abraham; they were "in the system," so to speak, while Melchizedek had no ancestral ties to Abraham. The idea being strongly presented here is that, because of this, Melchizedek stood *above* Abraham in rank, which is why Abraham gave him anything (7:6-7).[91] Melchizedek was a mortal man (7:8) but his office—its concept, symbolism, and foreshadow of that which was to come—remains forever fixed in time and history. "He lives on"—not literally, of course, since he *was* mortal, but figuratively in anticipation of the eternal office of Christ, the heavenly King-Priest.[92]

"And, so to speak, ...even Levi...paid tithes" (7:9-10)—in other words, if Abraham, from whom Levi descended, paid tithes to Melchizedek, then whatever priesthood is derived *through* Abraham (i.e., the Levitical priesthood) is also subordinate to Melchizedek's.[93] Thus, the dual-office nature of Melchizedek is greater than that of Levi and the priesthood bestowed upon his descendants. Furthermore, while Christ will copy the forms of the Levitical priesthood, He will more exactly occupy the same king-priest position of Melchizedek—making Him a *greater Priest* than any Levitical (high) priest. In fact, Christ is shown not to be just another copy of the heavenly pattern (like the tabernacle, priesthood, sacrificial system, etc.), but is *Himself* the pattern from which all such copies have originated.

---

91 The *tithe* and *blessing* are to be considered as one complete unit, much like *grace* and *faith*: Abraham was *blessed* because he offered a *tithe*. He would not have given tithes to a lesser man (who did not possess a blessing), nor would Melchizedek have blessed Abraham if he had withheld his tithe. The two actions go together and are not to be viewed separately.

92 It is this statement ("he lives on") and the one in 7:16 ("indestructible life") that have led some to assume that Melchizedek must be of divine origin, and that he is in perpetual existence, like Christ (John 8:58). Yet there is nothing in *Hebrews* or the rest of Scripture to validate such a bold claim or its serious implications.

93 Consider John the Baptist's reference to Jesus in John 1:30 as a related case in point.

The fact that God made Christ a High Priest of a new order necessarily implies the inadequacy of the first (Levitical) priesthood (7:11). And since the Levitical priesthood was ordained *through* the Law of Moses, a change in priesthood *necessarily demands* a change in law also. These two things (priesthood and law) cannot be separated: if one changes, so must the other (7:12). To underscore his point, the writer reminds his readers that Jesus did not descend from Levi, yet God declared Him to be "a great high priest" (recall 4:14). Several powerful conclusions are drawn from this simple fact (7:13-14):

- Jesus was not associated (hereditarily) with the Levitical priests but came from Judah, the tribe of kingship or royalty (see Gen. 49:10).
- The Law of Moses could not ordain anyone but a son (descendant) of Aaron to be high priest (Exod. 40:12-15, Lev. 8 – 9, etc.).
- Jesus did not minister to the physical temple to which the Levitical priests ministered.
- Jesus did not offer sacrifices on the altar over which the Levitical priests presided.
- Jesus' priesthood—its position, function, sacrificial system, etc.—is completely different and separate from that of the Levitical priests.

The two priesthoods, both being from God, cannot coexist for the same people (the Jews); the former must cease so that the latter may begin. In perfectly fulfilling the Law to which the priests ministered, Christ also made obsolete the function of its priesthood: all that the Law foreshadowed and prophesied (in its oracles and types) was summed up in Christ (Eph. 1:9-10). The objective having been fulfilled by Christ for the Law *and* its priests meant that they were no longer needed (Mat. 5:17). Those who would abandon Christ for the Law of Moses would be attempting to resurrect a system that God Himself had ended.[94]

---

[94] Perhaps the principle of the curse to rebuild what God has destroyed would apply to "rebuilding" the Law of Moses as it did to the rebuilding of Jericho (compare Josh. 6:26 and 1 Kings 16:34). Just as no man is to separate what God has joined together (Mat. 19:6, in principle), so no man is to resurrect what God has destroyed.

In contrast to the Levitical priests, Melchizedek's priesthood was not based on Abraham's lineage, Aaron's lineage, human genealogy, the Law of Moses, or anything that came after Abraham. It was already in existence when Abraham met him; Abraham had nothing to do with it. The "indestructible life [or, life indissoluble]" refers to the timelessness and (human) incorruption of Melchizedek's priesthood. This does not refer to Melchizedek himself but the symbolic character and dual-function of his office (7:15-16). Jesus did not resume Melchizedek's literal position but entered one *on the order* of it, according to its *likeness*. While Melchizedek's "life" (ministry) is indestructible in *type*, Jesus' life is *in fact* indestructible since He lives forever. Thus, Jesus brought to spiritual completion what Melchizedek's office could only foreshadow in a physical capacity. This was accomplished according to God's divine oath, not through the administration of men (7:17; citation is from Psalm 110:4).

The "former commandment" (i.e., Law of Moses) was "set aside" due to its "weakness" and "uselessness [or, unprofitableness]" (7:18). There was no defect or corruption in the Law itself—God does not give men defective or inferior laws (Rom. 7:12)—but it could not and was never *intended* to do what Christ alone could accomplish. The Law was "weak" in that it was *unable* to remove sin (Acts 13:38-39, Rom. 8:3, and Heb. 10:4). It was rendered useless (or obsolete) in that it has been fulfilled by Christ and thus superseded by a superior system of atonement *in* Christ. The Law, though ideal for its intended use, could not produce perfect men or a perfect priesthood (7:19).

Christ's Divine Ordination (7:20-22): God did not ordain Aaron and his sons as priests with a divine oath but according to the Law of Moses. In contrast, He has ordained His Son as an eternal High Priest with a divine oath or decree, not according to instructions and regulations set forth in a law given to men (7:20-21).[95] This further reveals the

---

95 God "will not change His mind" on this; or "will not repent" [KJV]. On this, Milligan aptly writes: "When God is said to repent, the meaning is that he simply wills a change; and when it is said that he will not repent, it means that he will never will a change. And consequently, there is nothing beyond the priesthood of Christ to which it will ever give place, as a means of accomplishing God's benevolent purposes in the

supremacy of Christ's office and His appointment to that office. The writer here introduces a new idea: since the Father has sworn Jesus in as an eternal High Priest, He (Jesus) also becomes the "guarantee" (i.e., promise, assurance, or surety) of a "better covenant" (7:22). Since Jesus' priesthood has rendered both the Law and its priesthood obsolete, it is *necessarily implied* that the covenant God made with Israel has been fulfilled.[96] Since it is fulfilled, it can no longer be workable or enforced; a "better covenant" has superseded it.[97]

The Law of Moses was not the fulfillment of God's promise to Abraham (Gal. 3:16-18) but only foreshadowed what was to come. The Levitical priesthood also was merely a shadow of things to come and not the very completion of God's "eternal purpose" (Eph. 3:11). In a sense, the Law and its priesthood served as one grand prophecy concerning the perfect dual-office of Christ the King *and* High Priest. "The value of the shadow lies in what it foreshadows; apart from this it would be empty, [and] was empty for all Jews who imagined the shadow to be the eternal substance and rejected the substance [Christ] as not being even a shadow but a grand delusion."[98]

---

redemption of mankind" (*Commentary*, 210).

96 This point undermines every claim that God still has some "unfinished business" with Israel, which is said will be completed during Jesus' alleged millennial reign on earth. On the contrary, Jesus' appointment as a new High Priest would be impossible unless *everything* God had promised Israel had already been fulfilled. Modern Premillennialists want to marry Christ's reign as King and High Priest with the future resurrection of the theocracy of Israel, but these two things are incompatible. If the one exists, the other cannot.

97 God's ultimate proof that His special relationship with Israel is over was demonstrated in His judgment against Jerusalem in AD 70 (see Luke 19:41-44, 21:20-24). That event destroyed the temple, which nullified sacrificial intercession, rendering the priesthood unworkable, and thus made obedience to the Law of Moses impossible.

98 Lenski, *Interpretation*, 230; bracketed words are mine.

Comparison of the Two Priesthoods
(7:23 – 8:13)

Aaron's priesthood was finite, limited in scope, and transitional (7:23). It was never meant to be held forever by one mortal man, nor could it be summed up *in* one man. The Levitical priests were "prevented by death" from serving perpetually: their deaths manifested an inherent limitation of their ability to serve perpetually. No matter how effective or instructive they might have been during their lives, they could only serve for a finite number of years. Their intercession between the people and God was limited; there was no perpetuity or continuity from one generation to the next.

Christ's Superior Priesthood (7:24-28): This is not the case with Jesus Christ, however (7:24-25). Just as His *life* (existence) is eternal, incorruptible, and unlimited in scope, His *priesthood* shares these same characteristics. Having conquered death to live eternally, Jesus unceasingly intercedes for His people ("He continues forever"). Also, Jesus' priesthood *is* summed up in one Man: Himself. Since He will not die, He has no heir-apparent, no replacement, and no successor. No one can terminate His office; no one can take away His life; He is unchangeable and indestructible (13:8). Since He forever *lives*, He forever *serves* His saints.

It was "fitting" [lit., suitable; proper; right[99]] for Christ to occupy the sublime role of an eternal High Priest (7:26-28). He is the ideal Person—indeed, the only *worthy* Person—who can fulfill every need of His people. More specifically, He is perfect for this role because He is:

- ❑ **"holy"**: sacred, pious, uncorrupted; having all the intrinsic divine qualities of the Father.[100] This refers to Jesus' internal character, as

---

99 James Strong, *Strong's Talking Greek-Hebrew Dictionary*, electronic edition (database © 2004 by WORDsearch Corp.), G4241.

100 Usually, "holy" is derived from *hagios*, which refers to the consecration of those who minister to God (as priests). Here, the word is *hosios* (Strong, *Dictionary*, G3741), which is similar in nature to *hagios*, but focuses upon one's personal sinlessness and

God has approved of Him.
- ❑ **"innocent"**: blameless, not having harmed anyone with injustice. This refers to Christ's relationship to law (guiltless) and to others (no cause for prosecution or restitution).
- ❑ **"undefiled"**: pure, untainted, and unblemished. This refers to Christ's having been a flawless offering, a perfect specimen, without any moral defect (see Lev. 22:17-25).
- ❑ **"separated from sinners"**: not, "having nothing to do with sinners" (else, He could not serve as our Advocate—1 John 2:1-2) but not worthy of a sinner's condemnation. He did not succumb to our crimes, illicit passions, or vices; He was tempted *with* sin but did not give Himself over *to* sin.
- ❑ **"exalted above the heavens"**: since Christ willingly humbled Himself on the cross, God proudly raised Him to the highest position in heaven (compare Isa. 52:13 and Phil. 2:6-9). He has no equal; none can compare to Him; He is unique in power and position (Eph. 1:21-22, 4:10); He sits at the right hand of the Father (Acts 2:33).
- ❑ **"who does not need daily ... to offer up sacrifices"**: the repetitive offering of sacrifices for their sins only underscored the fact that the Levitical priests were incapable of *perfectly* fulfilling the office to which they were appointed.[101] In other words, they were sinners just as were those for whom they interceded. Christ needs no personal purification; He *is* perfectly capable; He *does* perfectly fulfill His office. He can perfectly intercede for imperfect people since He is without sin (2 Cor. 5:21, 1 Peter 2:21).

---

piety (Wuest, *Word Studies*, 138; Robertson, *Word Pictures*, 386).

101 Nowhere in the Law was the high priest *specifically* to "offer up daily" a sacrifice for his own sins. However, the daily (morning and evening) sacrifices that the priests were required by Law to offer easily explains that to which the writer refers (Num. 28:1-8). While the emphasis of those sacrifices was on consecration (as "burnt offerings"), they were still considered bloody offerings. This blood was poured out at the base of the bronze altar as a means of atonement for sins. These sins must have to do with the priesthood, since the purpose of these offerings was to rededicate (daily) the tabernacle *and* those who ministered to it, so that both could be used to intercede for the people. In any case, the real sense of "daily" is that of repetitive action (McClister, *Commentary*, 269).

- ❑ **"once for all"**: lit., "once, without need or possibility of repetition" or "once, finally." This indicates the termination of any previous system, since this one absolutely and completely does what no other system could do. There will be no future high priest; there will be no other priesthood; "once for all" indicates finality and totality.[102] "The High Priest we should have is one who is not constantly under necessity of offering up sacrifices but one who once for all completes the sacrificial work by one all-sufficient sacrifice."[103]
  - Christ has been in the flesh once—He will not do it again (Heb. 9:26, 2 Cor. 5:16).
  - Christ suffered for human sins once—He will not do it again (1 Peter 3:18).
  - Christ died once—He will not do it again (Heb. 9:28).
  - The faith (i.e., gospel of Christ) was delivered once—it will not be delivered [by God] again (Gal. 1:6-9, Jude 1:3).
  - Christ offered His blood in heaven once—it will not have to be offered again (Heb. 9:12, 26).

The Law, perfect as it was for the purpose it served, nonetheless appointed weak men to minister to it (7:28). Again, it was unable to make men perfect; the best it could do was to define righteousness (and thus magnify sin) and condemn violators of that righteousness. On the other hand, God's divine oath has appointed an infinitely powerful, eternal, indestructible, and invincible High Priest "made perfect forever." *This* High Priest forgives people based upon His own authority and the perfect sacrifice of His own body and blood.

At the Right Hand of God (8:1-6): "Now the main point..."—lit., "the crown of things spoken previously" (8:1). The emphasis is not simply, "There *exists* such a High Priest," but that we *have* such a High Priest *actively interceding for all believers*. No common Israelite could have had

---

102 The fact that we are in the "last days" (Heb. 1:2) confirms this: there will not be another (new) dispensation in which we will need a different priest(hood), and thus a different law. What we have in Christ is final, all-sufficient, and will continue until the literal end of time.

103 Lenski, *Interpretation*, 244.

such personal intercession from the high priest of Israel; no high priest would have ever devoted such individual attention to him. But there is nothing "common" about being a Christian, since we have access to the "throne of grace" (recall 4:16) upon which sits *our* King of kings and our eternal High Priest—*our* King, *our* Priest! Aaron never reigned at the right hand of God but merely served a primitive role as an earthly servant of Jehovah. Yet Jesus has "taken His seat" alongside the One who has given Him all power and glory (recall 1:3).

Christ serves as a "minister in the sanctuary and in the true tabernacle"—these are earthly figures that symbolize heavenly realities (8:2). We are not to think that there is a giant tent-like sanctuary in heaven like the one that Moses constructed on earth. The writer only alludes to what (physical) structures we *do* know—in this case, the Mosaic tabernacle—to teach the spiritual lesson. Christ serves in God's world, in His heaven, in the very Presence of the Father. In this sense alone, He is vastly superior to any Levitical priest, who merely served a physical structure and ventured only once a year into the Holy of Holies, the innermost sanctuary of the tabernacle where the ark of the covenant was kept.[104] The "true tabernacle" is spiritual in nature, just as the believer's "true circumcision" (Phil. 3:3) is spiritual and not physical. In essence, God Himself is the spiritual "tabernacle," just as we are instructed elsewhere (Rev. 21:22; see Heb. 9:11, 24).

A high priest who has no sacrifices or gifts to *offer* completely fails in his responsibility as a *priest* (8:3). Likewise, Christ must have something to offer—something superior to whatever was offered under the Levitical system (since His office is superior to it). Indeed, He has offered that which no Levitical high priest could have possibly offered: His own uncorrupted life and sinless blood (Heb. 9:14). Notice the contrasts here (8:4):[105]

> "If He were on earth"—**but** *He is "in the heavens"*
> "He would not be a priest"—**but** *"we have such a high priest"*

---

104 This was done during the Day of Atonement; see Lev. 16.
105 Kistemaker, *NTC*, 218.

Earthly priests merely follow the patterns and instructions given them; otherwise, they would violate the very law that ordained them and to which they minister (8:5). These physical "copies" and "shadows" point forward to heavenly realities—something *outside* of themselves. While we might think that the heavenly tabernacle is a perfection of the copy, it is quite the opposite: Moses' tabernacle is a copy of the perfection. In other words, the earthly forms are patterned after what already exists in heaven, not the other way around. Just as Moses was given a "pattern" to follow (see Exod. 25:9, 40, and Acts 7:44), whatever was built according to that pattern could never be more than a representation of what already existed.

The writer summarizes his thoughts by reiterating the supremacy and majesty of Christ over all that has preceded Him (8:6):

- ❏ **"a more excellent ministry"**: a ministry superior to that of the Levitical priests in every sense and every function. While men minister from earth and offer earthly sacrifices, Christ ministers from heaven, having offered Himself to God and continuing to offer spiritual gifts to His people.
- ❏ **"mediator of a better covenant"**: superior to that which God made with Israel. That first covenant served as the basis for this new covenant; it was necessary for the one to exist first to prepare men for what was to come. Christ makes effective this new covenant, as we will see later in this epistle.
- ❏ **"[a covenant] enacted on better promises"**: the "better promises" of the eternal covenant transcend the physical world and its concerns, since it deals primarily with the salvation of men's souls. This is not to say that it does not govern the physical life (for it certainly does) but that it is designed to safeguard men *beyond* this life (Col. 3:1-4).

Everything in Christ is "better" than anything that has preceded Him, "better" than anything else we will ever have available on this earth. "Better" here does not mean merely better by comparison, but *the best that there is.*

The New Covenant (8:7-13): A covenant is an agreement between two parties to form a relationship with mutually beneficial objectives. It is not merely a contract, which focuses only on a particular thing or work being performed but creates a relationship that did not previously exist. A covenant does at least two things. **First**, it defines the relationship itself through its wording and the description of the roles of the two (or more) parties coming together in agreement. **Second**, it gives life (or functionality) to the relationship, making it operable, productive, and mutually rewarding. In other words, things can now be accomplished *because* of the relationship that could never be done *outside* (or in the absence) of it.

The only reason for God to make a covenant with people is to provide a means of fellowship that can overcome human sin. One who has never sinned against God does not need a covenant of salvation with Him.[106] Salvation—the act of being *saved* from something, in this case God's condemnation because of sin—is only necessary when one is in trouble, not when he is already innocent, safe, and in fellowship with the Lord. No one is invited into a covenant with God until or unless he has sinned; otherwise, his "salvation" is unnecessary. (This would be like doing surgery and putting a cast on an arm that is perfectly healthy.) God's covenants with people allows them to have fellowship with Him even though they have sinned against Him. There are provisions in the covenant that deal with those sins, as well as sins that will be committed in the future.

God's covenant with Israel (the two parties coming together in agreement) focused on the earthly concerns, such as family lineages (bloodlines), land inheritance, rightful dealings with fellow Israelites, ritual observances, festivals, etc. It had nothing to do directly with

---

[106] It is true that Jesus was circumcised on the eighth day, thus inducting Him into God's covenant with Israel (Luke 2:21). But this covenant was a *national* covenant, not a *personal* one; all its promises were meant for the Israelite community (see Deut. 28:1-14, for example), not solely for the individual believer. In other words, Jesus did not subject Himself to God's covenant with Israel because He was a sinful person but because He was indeed *an Israelite*, "born of [an Israelite] woman, born under the Law" (Gal. 4:4).

eternal life (although clearly those who were faithful to God's covenant on earth were blessed by Him in the life to come). God allowed the nation of Israel, through covenant, to have fellowship with Him *if* they remained faithful to that covenant. (In that covenant were stipulations for what this meant as well as spelled-out consequences for violations of it; see Deut. 28:15-68, for example.)

God's covenant with believers today is not a national covenant or even a group covenant: God has not made a covenant with America, for example, and He does not have a covenant with His church. Instead, a covenant is agreed upon between Him and *every individual believer*—it is a very personal covenant and thus a very personal relationship. We are not inducted into Christ's church in the same way that an Israelite was inducted into the Israelite community. Upon our personal, individual agreement to God's covenant of salvation—culminating in our baptism—we are thus added to the sanctuary of all *other* believers who have already done the same thing (Acts 2:41, 47). Technically speaking, we are baptized *into Christ*—into a covenant with God *through* Christ—and then are made part of His "body" (His church) *because* of this baptism (our agreement to this covenant of salvation).

When comparing the two covenants—God's covenant with Israel and His covenant with Christians—we must be careful not to misrepresent the first to justify the second. The first covenant was not "faultless," but it was not defective, either. God does not make defective or inferior covenants with men; whatever He does, it is perfect for the situation at hand. The problem was not the covenant itself, but Israel (the "them" in 8:8) in that they were unable (and often unwilling) to keep that covenant perfectly. Moreover, there was no means within the covenant itself to justify those who had violated it; this was its "fault" (or limitation). The covenant was perfect for that for which it was intended but looked *outside of itself* for its own completion.

This completion came through the establishment of a "new covenant"—one that rests upon the perfect obedience of *Christ* (not believers) and in which justification *is* possible. The illustration of a caterpillar-to-butterfly transformation is effective to explain this: the caterpillar is an ideal creature for the time being, but its purpose is not to remain a caterpillar but to become a butterfly. The caterpillar must look *outside of itself*—that is, outside of its present circumstances—to reach its full potential. At the same time, the butterfly cannot come into being without having begun as a caterpillar. Thus, each phase is mutually dependent upon the other. Interestingly, a kind of "death" must occur to make the caterpillar-to-butterfly transition, just as Jesus had to die to bring to completion the first covenant *and at the same time* inaugurate the "new covenant."

The passage in 8:8-12 is quoted from Jer. 31:31-34.[107] God made a covenant with Israel based upon external laws, rituals, and regulations (Deut. 5:1-3) but they continually violated this agreement. One stipulation in that covenant was that God would bring them to judgment through punishments and exile for these impenitent violations. Jeremiah, however, spoke of a future time when God would make a *new* covenant with Israel—*not* merely a recitation or reactivation of the *old* covenant but a *better* (superior) one.[108] Instead of focusing merely on external laws and regulations, this new covenant would be governed internally—i.e., through the indwelling of God's Holy Spirit (Rom. 8:9, 1 Cor. 6:19-20, Gal. 5:16, etc.).

From Jeremiah's day to the time of Christ, the Jews followed and served under the *old* covenant since the new one had not yet been revealed or put into effect. But in Jesus Christ, the new covenant is available to all people. This new covenant makes the old one obsolete; God does not offer two simultaneous (and competing) covenants to His people. Thus, one can never be right with God by abiding by a covenant He has made

---

107 Slight differences to the text in *Jeremiah* are because the writer of *Hebrews* quotes from the Septuagint rather than quoting from the Hebrew Bible. This is the case in virtually every OT citation in this epistle.

108 By quoting Jeremiah—one of the Jews' own prophets—to underscore the present point is "an astute move." The *Hebrews* writer "puts the Jewish recipients of this letter in the place where they will have to accept the New Testament and the testimony of their own prophet to the effect that…if they reject the New Testament, they will be forced to reject their own prophet" (Wuest, *Word Studies*, 143-144).

obsolete.[109]

- ❑ **"days are coming"** (8:8): This speaks of an indefinite timeframe but certainly future in its fulfillment. In OT language, this phrase often refers to the messianic age. Daniel is more specific (2:44), "In the days of those [Roman] kings...." The important factor (to Jeremiah's listeners) is not *when* this promise will be fulfilled but that it is divinely predicted and will most certainly *be* fulfilled.
- ❑ **"a new covenant"** (8:8): Again, this is not a mere renewal or resurrection of the old covenant.[110] This covenant was "new" in:
  - history (as an event).
  - time (relative to the "old" or "first" covenant).
  - people (all ethnicities are invited versus only Israelites; also, individual people are invited versus an entire nation).
  - scope (eternal life versus earthly life).
  - nature (spiritual realm versus physical realm).
  - mediation (Jesus Christ versus mortal priests).
  - ability (immediate forgiveness versus anticipation of a perfect sacrifice).
  - terms, conditions, and stipulations (lifestyle, requirements, expectations, etc. revealed in the gospel versus those outlined in the Law of Moses).
  - recording (on one's heart versus tablets of stone—Exod. 34:27-29, 2 Cor. 3:3).
  - blood (of Jesus versus the blood of animals).
  - blessings and curses (affecting one's eternity versus one's earthly circumstances or inheritance).
- ❑ **"the house of Israel and ... Judah"** (8:8): This is not a reference to a renewed or reunified physical kingdom, but a renewed *people*

---

109 This is underscored in Paul's comparison of the child of the bondwoman (i.e., Ishmael by Hagar) and the child of the free woman (i.e., Isaac by Sarah) in Gal. 4:21-31. The Jews wanted to cling to that which was passing away—i.e., the old system: the Law, Jerusalem, the temple system, etc.—while Christ is of the new and heavenly system. Those who cling to the earthly system cannot be heirs of the heavenly promises.

110 The word for "new" here in the Greek is *kainos*, which means new in design, freshly made, recently made, etc. (Thayer, *Lexicon* [electronic], G2537) rather than *neos*, which means "new" in time or sequence.

gathered in a completely new *context* (spiritual versus physical, political, or geographical). Israel and Judah are given priority invitation into this covenant (Rom. 1:16, Acts 3:25-26, and 13:46) but it is not exclusive to them. Furthermore, Israelites who reject this invitation forfeit all that it offers them.

- **"not like the covenant …"** (8:9): This new covenant is *based upon* the old one (in sequence, as well as fulfillment of types and symbols of the first) but is entirely new. That first covenant was established in a very primitive manner—with fire, smoke, thunder, and the sprinkling of animal blood—but this new covenant is established amid heavenly glory in the presence of God (to be covered in Heb. 12:18-24). That first covenant dealt with an earthly Promised Land, but this new covenant deals with a Sabbath rest in a heavenly "land" (Heb. 4:9 and 11:13-16).
- **"for they did not continue in My covenant …"** (8:9): The analogy to a marriage here is appropriate; the original Hebrew text for Jer. 31:32 appeals to such a relationship. Israel was like an unfaithful wife to Jehovah.[111] In a real sense, God divorced Israel for her unfaithfulness but now seeks a new relationship with believers (Jer. 3:1-10, Hos. 2:1-13). This is achieved in the "marriage" between Christ and His church, which serves as the heavenly pattern for earthly marriages (Eph. 5:22-27, Rev. 19:7-9).
- **"For this is the covenant that I will make …"** (8:10-11): Some notable contrasts between these two covenants include:
  - God's laws will not be merely written on scrolls or stone or kept as part of Israel's holy relics (Deut. 10:2) but will be "written" on the heart of every believer. This is not a new idea (see Deut. 6:6) but is given new significance here.
  - God's people will have a new identity—both individually (as Christians) and collectively (as Christ's church)—since they enjoy a new relationship with Him through Christ. The expression "I will be their God, and they will be My people" is

---

[111] "This point was appropriate to the original readers of Hebrews. To turn away from God through Christ would be to act just as the sons of Israel of old had acted: unfaithfully, rebelliously (see Heb. 10:29), turning to vanity, and refusing what God had offered them. If they acted just like the old Israel, they could have no part in God's covenant with the new Israel" (McClister, *Commentary*, 288-289).

not new but in Christ is taken to an entirely new level.[112]

- Under the old covenant, an infant male was circumcised on his eighth day to include him as a member of the covenant society. Females had no physical identity with the covenant, and even the eight-day-old males had no clue what was happening. In other words, sons had to be taught over time what it meant to be an Israelite and were dependent upon their fathers to teach them (Deut. 6:7). Now, however, people can learn the gospel anywhere, that is, from any person, at any place, in any nation, at any time. Anyone can "know the Lord," not only those whose fathers or families are already faithful.[113] Also, women are included in the covenant as equal heirs (Gal. 3:28-29). Thus, this new covenant transcends all the barriers imposed by the first covenant: race, gender, family ties, geography, government, and political boundaries.

❑ **"For I will be merciful ... and I will remember their sins no more"** (8:12): This means nothing less than complete and absolute remission of sins.[114] A soul can now stand before God without

---

112   In fact, this phrase resonates throughout the entire Bible: Exod. 6:7, Lev. 26:12, Jer. 31:33, 2 Cor. 6:16, Rev. 21:3, etc. What God has always wanted—and continues to seek—is a loving relationship with those who believe in Him. This objective is paramount to all other objectives; it is the underlying motive for all God has done in bringing salvation to mankind.

113   "To know the Lord is not to know about him, but to enter into a personal relationship with him, to know him intimately, to know his ways, his mind, his likes and dislikes, his intentions, and his character" (McClister, *Commentary*, 291).

114   Due to a misunderstanding of this verse, many Christians think that God literally *forgets* about our sins. Given God's divine nature—He knows *everything* and forgets *nothing*—this cannot be true. If there are facts, historical information, or *any* information outside of His knowledge, then He cannot be "God," as there would be something more powerful than Him that prevents Him from knowing this information. When God says "I will remember" (see Gen. 9:16, Exod. 6:5, and Lev. 26:45 for example) or "I will *not* remember," He is not saying, "I will suddenly recall what I had forgotten" or "I will forget this ever happened." Instead, He is saying, "I will take *action* on what has been said (or promised or done in the past)" or "I will *not* take action" on something that He knows *has* happened. An excellent example of this is in Jesus' parable of the unmerciful slave (Mat. 18:23-35). That slave was forgiven by the king—it could be said that the king "remembered this man's debt no more." But after hearing of the slave's unmerciful treatment of a fellow slave, the king *reinstated* the debt and held him accountable to pay it back in full. Jesus ended that parable by saying "My

condemnation (Rom. 5:1-2), being forgiven of his transgressions through the blood of Christ (Eph. 1:7). The old covenant "remembered" sins every year with every sin offering made (a reference to the Day of Atonement sacrifice in Lev. 16); it could only remove these sins through the promise of a future, all-sufficient sacrifice.

The "new" covenant demands that the "old" covenant be removed or made obsolete (8:13). The writer speaks of it in a gradual sense, however: "growing old" and "ready to disappear [or, near to vanishing away]." The reality of its obsolescence (i.e., its outdatedness or non-functionality) was apparent to those first-century readers who were paying attention to the signs of the times (Mat. 24:1-14). God allowed a 40-year transition period between the two covenants, giving time for the Jews throughout the world to hear the gospel of Christ. (Remember that the "new" covenant is new *to the Jews in particular*, as a fulfillment of what they were promised in the "old" covenant [8:10].) In just a few years (AD 66-70), when Judea revolted against Rome and Jerusalem fell to the Roman army, the 40-year transition would be complete. At that time, all the functional elements of the Law were destroyed, and it was very clear that God had permanently removed the old system.

A New Covenant in Christ's Blood (9:1-22)

To highlight the supremacy of Christ's priesthood over that of the Levitical system, the *Hebrews* writer now compares the role of the high priest in the Mosaic tabernacle with what Christ has done in the heavens. The Levitical high priest ministered within a physical-based system that merely reflected heavenly designs. The best he could do to intercede for Israel was to enter the throne room of God within that

---

heavenly Father will also do the same to you" if anyone does not forgive his fellow believer. Just because crimes are forgiven does not mean they are literally forgotten from memory. Likewise, the debt of our sin is not literally forgotten, but it is forgiven *if* we maintain the conditions by which this forgiveness was offered in the first place. See Bruce's comments (*Commentary*, 175-176) for a comparable explanation.

tabernacle—the Holy of Holies. Christ, however, entered the *literal* presence of God and presented Himself *in person* to intercede for all who identify with Him.

The Original Tabernacle as a Type Prophecy (9:1-10): Yet even though the first tabernacle was a physical, man-made structure (see Exod. 25 – 27), it still bore the imprints of heavenly concepts and ideas. It manifested heavenly *realities* through physical *symbols* or *representations* (9:1-5). As one scholar observes, "It is plain enough that 'the tabernacle' is used here symbolically for the whole system of Jewish worship."[115] The "outer" tabernacle refers to the Holy Place, the first room one encountered when entering the sanctuary. This room held three pieces of holy furniture: the golden altar (a.k.a. altar of incense), the seven-lamped candelabra, and the table of showbread.[116] Beyond this was the innermost sanctuary, known as the Most Holy Place or Holy of Holies, in which (in the original tabernacle) was kept only the ark of the covenant.[117] A heavy and richly ornamented veil separated the two rooms.[118]

---

115   Milligan, *Commentary*, 250.

116   At first glance, it appears that the writer says (in 9:4) the altar of incense was located *within* the Holy of Holies, when in fact it was not (Exod. 30:6, 40:26). Certainly, he was not confused, having already demonstrated his expertise in these matters. The seeming contradiction can be easily remedied by understanding that the altar of incense was so closely connected with the Holy of Holies, it was identified with it (1 Kings 6:22). "Having" a golden altar implies this close and necessary connection (Bruce, *Commentary*, 186). And, to access the Holy of Holies, the high priest had to first burn incense on the golden altar (Lev. 16:12-13): the one was necessary to partake of the other. See Lightfoot's expanded notes on this subject (*Jesus Christ Today*, 178-179).

117   Solomon's temple also had two huge statues of cherubim in the Holy of Holies (1 Kings 6:23-28).

118   The first veil was the one at the entrance to the first (or outer) sanctuary; the "second veil" (9:3) is the one between the first sanctuary and the second sanctuary, which is the Holy of Holies.

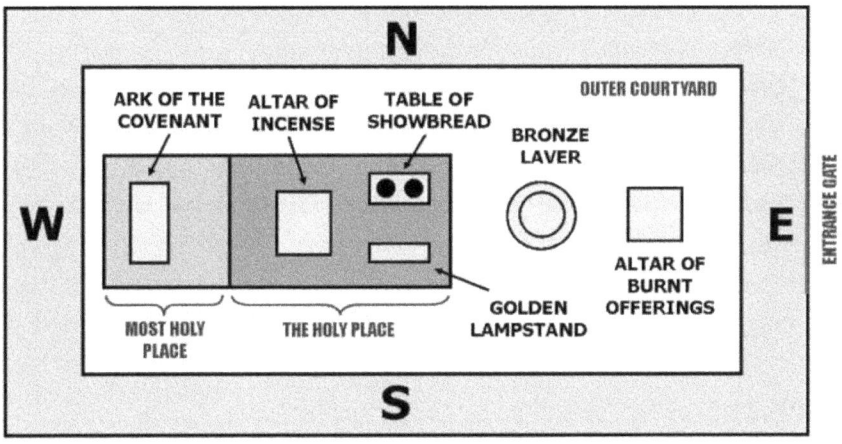

In Moses' day, the ark of the covenant resided in the Holy of Holies and contained a jar of manna (Exod. 16:33), Aaron's almond rod which had budded miraculously (Num. 17:8ff), and the tablets of the covenant (Deut. 10:1-5).[119] By Solomon's day, only the tablets of the Law remained (1 Kings 8:9, 2 Chron. 5:10). By Jesus' day, the ark of the covenant had long since disappeared; no one knows exactly what happened to it (see Jer. 3:16).

On top of the ark were two cherubim (guardian angels) which faced each other, the tips of whose wings touched each other (Exod. 25:10-22). The space directly above the ark, between the two angels, was purposely left empty, symbolizing the Presence of God which could not be formed into an image or shape (Exod. 20:4), except when God manifested Himself there as a "cloud" (see Lev. 16:2).[120] (The image here is a dramatic re-creation, not necessarily a literal rendition.)

---

119 Some believe the rod of Aaron was set *beside* the ark, given Num. 17:10, but we have no reason to dispute what is written here in 9:4.

120 This cloud was known as the *shekinah* ("glory of the Presence"), a word not found in the Hebrew Bible but used in extra-biblical rabbinic writings to describe God's ethereal presence (Exod. 40:34-35, 1 Kings 8:10-11).

The lid of the ark was called the "mercy seat" which was sprinkled with blood once a year to atone for the sins of the nation of Israel (9:5). In one sense, the ancient high priest was separated from the tablets of the Law (within the ark) by this mercy seat; only blood could serve as the *justifying* or *atoning agent* to reconcile the priest (who represented all of Israel) and God's Law. In a related sense, God ruled Israel from this "throne," while the high priest entered the Holy of Holies and served as an intercessor between Him and His people. "But of these things we cannot now speak in detail"—for one, because the originals did not exist any longer; for another, because the writer does not want his readers to focus on *signs*, but only uses them to draw attention to *substance*, which is Christ (Col. 2:16-17).

The priests daily used the outer sanctuary of the tabernacle to light the candelabra and burn incense for the daily sacrifice (9:6; see Exod. 30:7-8). Also, every Sabbath the bread on the table of showbread was replaced with twelve fresh loaves (Lev. 24:5-9). But the Holy of Holies was accessed only once a year on the Day of Atonement and *only with blood* (9:7; see Lev. 16). It was here, only on this day and only through the high priest, that the sins of the nation of Israel were removed year by year; otherwise, the tabernacle would be unclean, invalidating all individual offerings for sins on its altar. Without blood—a life offering—the high priest had no permission to enter God's presence and faced divine execution (Lev. 16:2).

The Holy Spirit has revealed these things in Scripture to teach us important lessons (9:8; see Rom. 15:4).[121] The way into the Holy of Holies—in reality, access to the heavenly presence of God—was shrouded in mystery and obscured from human vision, even while the actual tabernacle (temple) remained in Jerusalem.

> The [Spirit's] purpose was to show dramatically the darkness of the Jewish institution. The people, even though they were God's chosen people, could not enter even the sanctuary,

---

121 "The writer states that the Holy Spirit is both the divine Author of the Levitical system of worship and its Interpreter" (Wuest, *Word Studies*, 154).

to say nothing of the holy place where God's presence was symbolized. Only a relatively few priests could enter, and even they were excluded from entering within the veil, where only one of them, the high priest alone, might enter under the most limited circumstances, and upon only one day in the year. And even when the high priest entered, the mercy-seat was first covered with smoke of incense, showing that, even after all the ritual, God would not really look upon the high priest, except as through the smoke that screened his unworthiness from the Lord.[122]

Nonetheless, the physical structure still served as "a symbol for the present time" (9:8)—in other words, it continues to teach lessons. One such lesson: if access to God had been fully realized through the *old* system, there would be no need for a veil or separation within the temple. The fact that it physically remained (at the time this epistle was written) indicated the *incompleteness* of that system. A better one was needed (and indeed now exists) if that separation was to be removed. Not even the forms and regulations (or gifts and sacrifices) of the old system could cleanse the human conscience; physical rituals cannot overcome spiritual deficiencies (9:9-10); the blood of an irrational animal cannot remove the sins of a rational being. Nonetheless, these things pointed forward to a "time of reformation" or "a new order" or "times of refreshing" (Acts 3:19).[123] "What he means is that unimpeded access to the presence of God was not granted until Christ came to accomplish His sacrificial ministry."[124]

Christ's Presentation in the Spiritual Temple (9:11-14): "But when Christ appeared..." (9:11-12)—this indicates a change of status and the supersession of the old system (compare with Titus 3:4-7). Christ's

---

122 Coffman, *Commentary*, 193-194.

123 "The word [for "reformation"—*diorthosis*] in its context here means 'to bring matters to a satisfactory state'" (Wuest, *Word Studies*, 156; bracketed words are mine). This necessarily implies that old (Jewish) system was less-than-satisfactory and was set right by Christ's sacrifice. "'[A] time of reformation' (our versions) is not a satisfactory English rendering" (Lenski, *Interpretation*, 287).

124 Bruce, *Commentary*, 195.

entrance into the spiritual tabernacle (i.e., the Presence of God) was not accomplished through forms, symbols, or shadows. It is not of this world, just as His kingdom is not of this world (John 18:36). Instead, He entered this heavenly tabernacle; in so doing, He Himself is the reality and substance of our salvation—the "summing up of all things" (Eph. 1:9-10). His arrival was deliberate and purposeful: it was to present (through the historical event of His sacrificial death) His body and His blood as a sin offering for the whole world (1 John 2:2).[125]

Christ's presentation into the Presence of God followed the basic ritual of the Day of Atonement, but the Day of Atonement is a pale reflection of this scene, not the other way around. A noticeable difference, however, is that Christ did not offer a sacrifice first for His own sins, as was required of the ancient high priests (since He was sinless). Also, He did not atone for the sins of a given nation for a limited period (as the ancient high priests did). Instead, He secured "eternal redemption" for those who were thus cleansed by His blood (Rom. 5:9, Eph. 1:7, Col. 1:20, etc.).[126]

At this point (9:13-14), the writer alludes to a different sacrifice than the Day of Atonement (the offering of "bulls and goats"). The "ashes of a heifer" refers to the elaborate cleansing ritual (the so-called "red heifer ordinance"—see Num. 19) for those who had become defiled through contact with death (i.e., a dead body or a grave). In that ritual, a flawless red heifer was ceremonially slain and then burned to ashes; these ashes were mixed with water and then sprinkled upon the one defiled by death to cleanse him. (The full cleansing ritual took seven days to complete.)

---

125 "It is not of course meant that he literally *bore* his own blood into heaven—as the high priest did the blood of the bullock and the goat into the sanctuary...but that that blood, having been shed for sin, is now the ground of his pleading and intercession for the pardon of sin—as the *sprinkled* blood of the Jewish sacrifice was the ground of the pleading of the Jewish high priest for the pardon of himself and the people" (Barnes, *Notes*, 192).

126 "What a contrast between 'a brute beast slain involuntarily, without foreknowledge, and without capacity to consent to, or appreciate the reason of, its dying' and 'a holy, loving Man, who laid down His own life deliberately, freely, devotedly, animated by an eternal spirit of goodness'" (A. B. Bruce, *Hebrews* (1899), quoted in Lightfoot's *Jesus Christ Today*, 170).

Being defiled by death and being corrupted by sin are parallel situations: both make fellowship with God impossible.

If the blood or ashes of an animal can (ritually) cleanse the person defiled by sin or death, then the body of Christ can cleanse us absolutely. Animal blood is only a type of what God requires for the atonement of human sins; an animal's ashes can only ritually cleanse the human body, but they cannot cleanse the human soul or conscience. Yet Christ's offering does infinitely more than these: His "unblemished" body and innocent blood cleanse the human conscience of its sin and guilt (or condemnation).[127] No animal sacrifice can do this; not even a sinner's self-sacrifice could accomplish this. "The blood of Christ sets aside all other plans for pardon."[128]

We should not overlook the role of "{the} eternal Spirit" (9:14)—a unique expression in Scripture—in the process of one's spiritual cleansing.[129] God's Holy Spirit is the agent of sanctification (1 Cor. 6:11, 2 Thess. 2:13, and 1 Peter 1:2)—i.e., the process of making one holy to God. In other words, it is not Christ acting alone to bring about our cleansing; yet it is also impossible for the Holy Spirit to sanctify anyone who has not been sprinkled with Christ's blood. The Spirit did not die for us on the cross; yet Christ does not impart life apart from the power of God's Spirit (John 6:63).

Each Personage of the Godhead performs His appropriate function: God the Father wrote the Plan of Redemption and enacts it by His own sovereign authority; God the Son offered His body and blood to give life to this Plan; and God the Spirit calls the sinner into this Plan

---

127 This cleansing is not accomplished apart from the believer's own participation. In 1 Peter 3:21, for example, we learn that baptism (i.e., immersion in water) is the *believer's* role in cleansing his conscience. His is an act of faith; Christ's is an act of grace. Christ does not baptize people, and people cannot cleanse their own conscience apart from the sprinkling of His blood. Thus, Christ *and* the believer must act accordingly.

128 Robertson, *Word Pictures*, 403.

129 In the Greek text, there is no definite article ("the"), but it reads, "…who through eternal Spirit offered Himself…." This does not, in my understanding, invalidate the points being offered here on this phrase.

(2 Thess. 2:14) and sanctifies him once his sins have been forgiven. The "eternal Spirit" indicates the *power* behind Christ's ministry and thus the authority by which He offered Himself as an atoning sacrifice. Even in His earthly ministry, Christ did not act separately from the Holy Spirit, but it was the Spirit who is credited with the power of His miracles (Mat. 12:18, 28, Luke 4:14, Acts 10:38, etc.).

Ratification of the New Covenant (9:15-17): "For this reason" (9:15)—that is, since Christ has accomplished what no man, animal, ceremonial ritual, or earthly sacrifice could accomplish, the following facts are also true. Christ fulfills both sides of the high priest's function: He not only is the *intercessor*, doing what no other high priest could do, but He also is the *sacrifice*, offering what no other high priest could offer. His death redeemed all those faithful to the "first" covenant since His death was anticipated and made necessary *by* it. Thus, "the death of Christ is retroactive,"[130] just as we also see in Rom. 3:25. "The word *covenant* implies sin. Sin necessitates the making of a new covenant and the shedding of blood."[131] Thus, *all* who have sought salvation through covenant with God are saved indeed through Christ's blood, regardless of which specific covenant they were under.

The word "covenant" here [Greek, *diatheke*] can also be translated "will" or "testament," such as what one writes before he dies concerning the disposition of his estate. A testament does not have any legal force until the death of the one who makes it; thus, without that death, the inheritance remains in the hands of the testator (the author of the will). The analogy here is not perfect, nor was it meant to be, but is only an illustration of what has already been said. Just as a testament requires the death of the testator to *bring it to life*, so the new covenant required the death of Christ to *bring it to life*. "Those who have been called" refers to those who have been called by God through His promises to Israel or His promises of His gospel.[132] Those who are called by God must also

---

130 JFB, *Commentary* (electronic), on 9:15.

131 Kistemaker, *NTC*, 256.

132 Under the first covenant, physical (land) inheritance was crucial to the prosperity and continuity of the Israelite. Everything that identified him to God was somehow

call upon Him (compare Acts 2:21 and 2:39).

"For where a covenant is, there must of necessity be the death of the one who made it" (9:16). Again, the implication of a *testament* here is for illustrative purposes only; it is not an exact explanation of what has happened.[133] The reasons for this is because:

- The covenant is *God's*, not Christ's. Christ offers His blood as the "blood *of* the covenant" (Mat. 26:28, emphasis added) but nowhere is the covenant referred to as His own (see Heb. 12:24 and 13:20).
- The Father (the author of the covenant) did not die but His Son died. Some might say that (generally speaking) *God* died for us since the Word which became flesh is what was nailed to the cross (John 1:1-3, 14) but the context here in *Hebrews* is not talking in generalities. The writer consistently identifies God as the Father and Jesus Christ as the Son. God the Father is not *literally* a "testator" (one who makes a last will and testament) but is more accurately a *covenant-maker*.
- The Son does not offer the covenant, but His blood only legalizes or ratifies it. Just as the U.S. Constitution had no legal force (or "life") until ratified by those states that signed it, so God's covenant of salvation had no legal force (or "life") to cleanse the souls of men apart from the blood of Christ (9:17).

---

tied to the Promised Land, that gift which God provided for the Israelite to sustain him. But when the Israelite died, he left that inheritance to his posterity. For the believer in Christ, however, his inheritance is yet to come but is guaranteed by the power of his covenant with God in Christ (9:15). Just as the first covenant guaranteed the Israelite's land inheritance, so the "better covenant" guarantees a heavenly inheritance. In both covenants, inheritance is conditioned upon the believer's continued faithfulness.

133 It is unfortunate that we use "testament" rather than "covenant" to define the gospel message ("New Testament"). For one, "testament" is not as accurate as "covenant"; for another, if we spoke of the "New Covenant" (as Jesus did—Luke 22:20), then so much of the foreignness of our *relationship* with God would be removed, and we would emphasize this relationship so much more (versus focusing on the trappings and liturgy *of* that relationship—i.e., church services, church protocol, etc.). For a better understanding of "covenant," I recommend (but do not endorse every conclusion of) *God's Eternal Purpose and the Covenants* by Homer Hailey (Louisville: Religious Supply, 1998); and *The God of the Covenant* by David Lusk (Mesa, AZ: [self-published], 2002.

- ❏ Christ did indeed die but He also resurrected from that death. Normally, the testator dies, and his son receives the inheritance. Here it is reversed: the *Son* dies; then something unnatural happens—He rises again. And finally, not in this world but in the spiritual realm, He receives His inheritance.
- ❏ The Father does not disperse all things directly to believers but has given all things to His Son, who then *shares* His inheritance with those who believe in Him (Eph. 1:13-14).

Blood serves as the most important physical substance on earth because it contains within it the essence of life and God has given it for the very purpose of atonement (Lev. 17:10-11). Therefore, every legal transaction that requires God's justice toward a person's state of condemnation must be satisfied with blood (i.e., life for life).[134] Even the "first covenant" (God's covenant with Israel) was inaugurated with blood (9:18-20). After Moses set forth the essential terms of this covenant to the Israelites at Mt Sinai, the people declared that "All the words which the Lord has spoken we will do!" With that commitment, Moses offered burnt offerings and peace offerings to God, then took some of the blood from those offerings and sprinkled it upon the altar and then upon the people.[135] As he did so, he said, "Behold the blood of the covenant, which the LORD has made with you..." (Exod. 24:3-8).

---

134 Blood indicates the vicarious sacrifice of the one being offered. One life is given for another; the sinner lives only because of the life offered in his place. In the old economy (the Levitical system), an animal's life sufficed for this transaction; in the grand scheme of things, however, only the blood of a perfect Son of Man—One who was also the Son of God—could satisfy God's ultimate requirement for justice.

135 While that original account does not mention Moses literally sprinkling the "book" (i.e., the written detail of the covenant), this action can be easily implied (9:19). But the "water and scarlet wool and hyssop" combination seems to belong to a different occasion, either the red heifer ordinance (Num. 19:6, 18) or the ritual cleansing of a healed leper (Lev. 14:4, 6). It is possible that Moses used these elements in the inauguration of the covenant, and that the writer of *Hebrews* is drawing on sources unavailable to us today. Or it may be that he is incorporating several different facets of sacrifices involving *ritual cleansing* to illustrate the overall point: people cannot be cleansed apart from divine ordinances, and especially blood.

Later, upon its dedication, the tabernacle and all its furniture and implements were also sprinkled with blood (9:21; see Lev. 8:15 and 16:14-16). Even the sons of Aaron were cleansed (by daubing and sprinkling) with blood (Lev. 8:22-24, 30). "Almost" all things in the Law of Moses were cleansed with blood (9:22): a few exceptions involved water or fire as the cleansing agent. But one's induction into a covenant relationship *and* forgiveness of sins (atonement) were never accomplished apart from "shedding of blood."[136] "[W]ithout shedding of blood there is no forgiveness" is one of the most important points of this entire epistle.

Christ's Once-for-all Offering (9:23 – 10:18)

Earthly "copies" of heavenly things (i.e., the tabernacle and its furniture and utensils) could not address the full scope of what God required for spiritual atonement (9:23). Even so, these earthly copies needed to be cleansed (or purified) with blood, and animal blood was sufficient for such cleansing. Yet "better sacrifices" than animal blood and meal offerings were necessary for the redemption of human souls. Christ did not enter the *copy* of heavenly things (i.e., a man-made tabernacle) but heaven itself; His blood does not merely cleanse earthly elements of worship but cleanses the consciences of human souls for worship to God (9:24; see Col. 1:19-22 and 1 Peter 1:18-19).[137]

Before offering blood on behalf of the nation of Israel, the ancient high priest first had to offer blood to cover his own sins (9:25). Yet Christ,

---

136 Under the Law, a very poor man could bring a bloodless sin offering (Lev. 5:11-12) but the priest still had to make atonement for him (5:13), which necessarily implied a blood offering from another source. Ultimately, the Day of Atonement sacrifice would cover all such omissions. Thus, "the *memorial* was made with flour, but the *atonement* with blood" (Milligan, *Commentary*, 262; emphasis is his).

137 "It has frequently been asked in what sense the 'heavenly things' required to be cleansed; but our author has provided the answer in the context. What required to be cleansed was the defiled consciences of men and women; this is a cleansing which belongs to the spiritual sphere" (Bruce, *Commentary*, 218).

being sinless, did not have to offer blood for Himself nor did He have to offer Himself more than once. The writer proposes an absurd situation to make his point: if Christ's once-for-all offering was not sufficient, He would have had to offer Himself many times, from the beginning of time until the end of time (9:26).

But this is not necessary since His one offering satisfied all that God required for all time. This reveals how *valuable* and *powerful* His offering was: rivers of animal blood over many centuries could not compare to the outpouring of His blood on the cross. Out of billions of men who have ever lived, not one is worthy to do what He alone did (Rev. 5:1-10). (The "consummation of the ages" refers to the "last days"; see comments on 1:2.) While Christ does not "put away sin" against anyone's free will, His one offering is sufficient to deal with the sins of the entire world (John 1:29, 1 John 2:2).

The phrase "it is appointed for men to die once" (9:27) emphasizes the certainty and singular occurrence of one's death, not how or when he will die.[138] Just as men die once, so Christ died once; He does not have to keep dying over and over to sustain what His *one* death accomplished. While a person's death is inevitable, as the result of the curse against his physical *life* (Gen. 3:17-19, Rom. 8:10), Christ's death was self-determined and is life-giving, having overcome the curse (or condemnation) against the human *soul* (Rom. 8:1, Gal. 3:13). He "will appear a second time" (9:28) but not to die again.[139] This "second"

---

138 The "after this comes judgment" phrase (9:27) does not mean that judgment *immediately* follows (in time) but that it *follows* death (in sequence). "It simply means that judgment is the next significant thing that happens after death" (McClister, *Commentary*, 329).

139 What remains unfinished here is: what is meant by Christ's "second time" appearance? Some believe that the writer refers to Jesus' judgment against the Jewish nation, especially since this was soon to come in relation to the writing of this epistle. But while Jesus *was* to "appear" in judgment against Jerusalem (Mat. 24:29-31), this is not the only *kind* of "appearance" that is mentioned in Scripture. In fact, the *Hebrews* writer is specific: Jesus' second appearance will *not* be with reference to sin—which necessarily excludes His judgment against Israel since sin was the *only reason* for that appearance—but will be for salvation of believers. Sin must be dealt with before salvation is realized. This second appearance cannot be reduced to a metaphorical

appearance will be to bring into glory those who "eagerly await" Him (i.e., His faithful followers)—but also, it is implied, to bring judgment against those who have refused Him (see 2 Thess. 1:6-9).[140]

Animal Sacrifices Are Inferior to Christ's Sacrifice (10:1-4): "Law" here (10:1) refers to the Levitical sacrificial system and its ritual cleansing ordinances. These things were provided for *physical illustrations*; they were never meant to be taken as *spiritual truths*. They were *shadows* and *forms*, not the substance (Col. 2:16-17).[141] Animal blood could not redeem the human soul, no matter how many animals or how frequently ("year by year") they were offered. This does not mean that they were not important since God commanded that they be offered, and they did serve a divine purpose. No one who has sinned could (or can) draw near to God without a blood sacrifice to cover his sins.

The ancient Israelites, like Christians today, were justified by faith and saved by grace (Rom. 5:1-2, Eph. 2:8). They were not justified by repetitious blood sacrifices (10:2) any more than we are justified by repetitious churchgoing and hymn-singing. If the physical, blood sacrifices of animals were complete in themselves, then there would be no need to offer them over and over; a once-for-all offering would be

---

appearance but is a literal one to those who await Him (see Acts 1:11, 1 Thess. 4:13-18, 1 Peter 5:4, 1 John 2:28, 3:2, etc.).

140 Bruce offers a further perspective, corresponding to the ancient Levitical priesthood. "The Israelites who watched their high priest enter the sanctuary for them waited expectantly for his reappearance; that was a welcome sign that he and the sacrifice which he presented had been accepted by God. His reappearance from the holy of holies on the Day of Atonement was a specially [sic] welcome sight. ... So our author thinks of Jesus as going into the heavenly holy of holies, to reappear one day in order to confirm finally to His people the salvation which His perfect offering has procured for them" (*Commentary*, 223-224).

141 "Of these good things the law had but a shadow (*skia*), but with the coming of Christ the shadow gave way to the true form (*eikon*) of real things. The terms *skia* and *eikon* express the comparative worth of Leviticalism and Christianity. The *skia* is a dark outline, faint and indistinct, like an artist's first sketch of a picture; the *eikon* is the image itself, an exact representation, as an artist's finished portrait with all the colors in it" (Lightfoot, *Jesus Christ Today*, 183).

sufficient. The fact that they *were* offered repeatedly pointed forward to the perfection of what they only foreshadowed.[142] The people of Israel were never able to forget how far and how often they fell short of God's holiness since a multitude of sacrifices constantly reminded them of this (10:3). "For it is impossible for the blood of bulls and goats to take away sins" (10:4)—the writer could not have been clearer and more direct in his statement (see Acts 13:38-39). In sharp contrast, Christ's offering of Himself—and the blood He deliberately shed in doing so—*does* take away sins.

The Body of Christ's Sacrifice (10:5-10): In this next section, the focus is not really on the *act of the consummate offering* itself but the *body (of Christ) that was offered*. The quote from Psalm 40:6-8, a messianic passage, emphasizes this. Christ was not oblivious to His mission; He understood it completely.[143] He both came of His own volition *and* was sent to carry out the Father's "eternal purpose" (Eph. 3:11-12). He both knew and even orchestrated the events surrounding His own death (Mat. 16:21, John 10:17-18, etc.). He was given a body with which to serve this purpose: "the Word became flesh" (John 1:14). He could not be an appropriate offering for people without having a *human body*. Just as the bronze serpent in the wilderness was made in the likeness of the Israelite's affliction (Num. 21:6-9, John 3:14-15), so Christ came "in the likeness of sinful flesh and as an offering for sin" (Rom. 8:3).

In sum, Christ came "to do Your will, O God" (10:7). This commitment was not fulfilled after a period of mistakes or trial and error, a period of sober reflection (like what we naturally experienced during our own conversion), or with a slow but gradual realization of who He was and His otherworldly role. Jesus was never *converted* to becoming a disciple of God but was born as His Apostle (recall 3:1). He always lived in

---

142 Milligan suggests that there were multiple sacrifices offered daily, weekly, monthly, and yearly for the *same sins*. "On the tenth day of the seventh month [on the Day of Atonement], all the sins of the past year were again called into remembrance and an atonement made" (*Commentary*, 267-268; bracketed words are mine).

143 This, despite modern Hollywood attempts to portray Him as a torn, confused man who finds Himself caught up in circumstances beyond His control, such as Martin Scorsese's *The Last Temptation of Christ* (1988).

fellowship with His Father and always sought to please Him in all things (John 8:29).

We cannot read "sacrifice and offering You have not desired" (10:5) apart from its point of reference. This is a statement of *comparison* or *contrast*, not a renouncing or dismissal of all the ancient sacrifices. God *did* desire sacrifices and offerings—otherwise He never would have commanded them! Yet He is more pleased with human compliance to His requests for sacrifice than He is the death of animals. Even so, God ultimately sought something that mere animal sacrifices and ritual offerings could ever provide: a *perfect sacrifice* through the *willful obedience* of a perfect Man (10:6-7).[144] Things offered by Law (as part of the "first" covenant) could not accomplish this; thus, Jesus came to fulfill the first covenant and establish a "better" (superior) one in its place (10:8). This was meant to be because:

- it was prophesied that another lawgiver (i.e., of higher rank than Moses) would arise to give a superseding law (Deut. 18:15-19).
- the first covenant's priesthood was inherently limited by the priest's own sins; the corruption of the office by greed and politics; and death (requiring a successor).
- its elements of worship were earthly, man-made, and primitive.
- its tabernacle, and all its furniture, was only a copy (or "shadow") of the heavenly and thus could not be used to render heavenly verdicts.
- its sacrifices were inferior to what was required: the blood of animals cannot atone for human sins.
- it was made only with Israel, even though God desired for "all the families of the earth" to blessed through covenant (Gen. 12:3, Acts 3:24-26), which necessitated a single, universal covenant with all of humankind (Isa. 49:1-6, Eph. 3:1-12).
- the limitation of its practices prevented it from indefinite usage. In other words, this covenant became impractical as men multiplied and moved increasingly further away from the center of worship— Jerusalem and its temple. (In the new covenant, geography and historical places are no longer relevant; see John 4:21-24.)

---
144 This is also the ultimate implications in passages like 1 Sam. 15:22 and Mic. 6:7-8.

- the temple of God had been so corrupted, it warranted nothing short of destruction (Mat. 24:1-2, Luke 19:41-44, etc.), which meant it could not serve its original purpose forever.
- the entire covenant—its law, promises, and the terms and conditions of one's relationship with God—pointed forward to something *outside of itself* to finalize what it had begun.

The offering of the "body of Jesus Christ" (10:10) refers to nothing less than the literal, factual, historical act of Christ's death upon the cross. Sanctification (or holiness) is impossible apart from His bodily offering.[145] He could not have shed His blood if He did not have a body; His body would have been useless if not filled with life-giving blood. This unites Jesus the Son of Man (of earth) with Christ the Son of God (of heaven): His death accomplishes what was needed upon earth as well as in heaven. His death, being complete, perfect, unique, and all-sufficient, serves all people for all time: it is truly "once for all."

Christ's Offering Provides Absolute Forgiveness (10:11-18): The writer continues to contrast the work of the Levitical priest with that of Christ. The emphasis here (10:11) is on the priest who worked *standing up* and Christ who has *sat down*. Every Levitical priest *stood* to minister and offer sacrifices; he never ministered while sitting down. But despite all his standing and ministering, the sacrifices he offered could never "take away sins." Thus, despite his zealous devotion or reverent piety, there was an inherent futility to his work. "Time after time" seems to imply more than mere repetition; it also implies monotony and even exasperation. The prevalence of human sin and defilement forever required his services; he could never sit down (so to speak) because his work was never finished.

But Christ offered His *one sacrifice*, then "sat down at the right hand of God" (10:12; recall comments on 1:3-4). While the priests fearfully

---

[145] Sanctification is impossible, too, apart from the work of the Holy Spirit, as we have already discussed. But the Spirit could not do His work unless (or until) Christ has done *His* work. While the work of Christ *and* the Holy Spirit are essential in one's salvation, nonetheless it is Christ's work which must be applied first. No one can be sanctified to God until his sins have been dealt with properly and completely.

entered the Holy of Holies year after year, Christ fearlessly and triumphantly entered its *heavenly reality*—the *true* Holy of Holies, the very Presence of God Himself—and took His rightful seat as both King and High Priest of the kingdom of God. His earthly humility, ministry, bodily offering, and blood sacrifice were once and "for all time" behind Him; now He sits on His throne, exercising kingly authority and administering priestly intercession.[146]

There is another part of the great cosmic sequence, however, that has yet to be fulfilled: Christ still waits "until His enemies be made a footstool for His feet" (10:13; see Mat. 22:41-45 and 1 Cor. 15:23-26). His enemies are allowed to exist and (within their imposed boundaries) even enjoy a limited measure of success *for now*. The reasons for this include:

- God will allow them (Christ's enemies) time to prove their complete unwillingness to submit to Him on their own.
- In doing so, God will show Himself to be fair and just in His punishment of Christ's enemies, since they chose of their own free will not to repent of their sins and rebellion.
- This manifests His absolute power over these enemies—i.e., no matter how much time they are given to overwhelm Him, His power remains intact and undisturbed, and He cannot be defeated by any person or power that resists Him.

God will, in essence, put the necks of all of Christ's enemies "under His feet" (see comments on 1:13). This does not mean that Christ is powerless to do this Himself; the *idea* presented here is that God the Father will bring absolute justice to all those who refuse to honor the Son whom the Father has highly exalted (Phil. 2:9-11). This is a matter

---

146 There is no hint in Scripture that Jesus will reign in Jerusalem for a millennium, Rev. 20:4-5 notwithstanding. Christ's work on earth is done; "It is finished" (John 19:30). To claim that He needs to resume His earthly ministry to complete some unfinished business regarding God's kingdom and/or His promises to Israel is to undermine everything that He *did* accomplish. The implication of Premillennialism, then, is that Jesus failed to do what He (and the Father) set out to accomplish, yet nothing could be further from the truth.

of divine retribution: God cannot allow those who challenge His Son to go unpunished; He must and will defend His holiness through the destruction of those who offend it. This implies a word of warning, too, to the original readers of this epistle: if they make themselves to be enemies of God (through their disregard of His Son's offering), then they also will be the objects of divine wrath.

"For by one offering...for all time [lit., in perpetuity]" (10:14)—what Christ accomplished was all-sufficient and final. The Holy Spirit, the source of the prophecy quoted from Jer. 31:33-34, has "testified" or confirmed these things to us (10:15-17; recall 8:8-12).[147] Once again, the writer makes a necessary connection between the *blood offering* and *covenant*. God could not have made a covenant with us apart from Christ's blood; yet forgiveness of sins is only obtained through entering a covenant relationship with God. Since those who *are* in covenant with God are forgiven absolutely, there is no need for a further sin offering (10:18).

---

147 This is like what Paul wrote in Rom. 8:16-17. The Holy Spirit testifies *with* us concerning our salvation, if indeed we do what He has instructed us.

Section Four: The Need for Greater Faith and Endurance (10:19—12:29)

Third Warning against Apostasy (10:19-39)

What follows here is a connection of thoughts from 4:14-16 and 9:13-14 but for a new emphasis: *the believer's confidence.* While the unconverted Jews longed to enter the "holy place" within the literal Jerusalem temple, the Christian has *confidence* to enter something infinitely greater—holy throne room of God Himself. This is not something he does in person but is accomplished through what *Christ* did personally. The writer explains this in human terms, however, by referring to His physical body ("flesh") and blood (10:19-20). The reason for this is because the two are necessarily related: Christ could not have presented Himself before the Father without the historical reality of His bodily offering and the willful shedding of His blood.

A New and Living Way to God (10:20-23): "Through the veil" (10:20) is an allusion to the literal veil (heavy curtain) between the two sanctuaries of the temple. Through that veil the high priest accessed the Holy of Holies. But God has torn that veil in half upon the death of His Son (Mat. 27:51) and has given us access to Him in the Spirit (Eph. 2:18). Instead of attempting to draw near to God through the old system of physical rites and animal sacrifices, we have a "new and living way" by which to fellowship with God (10:20).[148] Thus, "every Christian

---

148 The word "new" here is from *prosphatos* (Strong, *Dictionary*, G4372), which literally means "newly slain" or "freshly slaughtered" (Wuest, *Word Studies*, 179). Clearly, the implication here is that Jesus' sacrificial death opened an entirely new

now has the privilege that was once reserved for the high priest. The Christian can do, at any time, what the high priest could do only once a year."[149] Besides, the old system would soon be destroyed (by AD 70); its sacrifices were no longer effective; its priesthood has been superseded by the high priesthood of God's Son. Not only is there nothing to which the Hebrew Christians could return, there are *excellent reasons* why they should have confidence and "full assurance" to continue forward with Christ.

Given all that Christ has done, "we have confidence" to do what men before either feared to do or were prevented from doing. We do not merely have "a" priest, but we have—to our great advantage—a "great high priest" who serves as a forerunner for us. He does not minister to a physical temple on earth but presides over "the [heavenly] house of God" and is the head of the spiritual church of God (10:21; see Eph. 2:19-22 and 1 Peter 2:4-5). Therefore, instead of drawing *away* from Christ (as the Hebrew Christians were contemplating), the writer gives reasons why believers should draw near to God *through* Christ (10:22). This should be done "in full assurance of faith" because of what Christ has done as an act of divine grace: He has sprinkled our souls with His blood, purging us of an "evil" conscience (recall 9:13-14; see 1 Peter 1:2).

But this "[drawing] near" is also because of what each believer has done in human faith: he has been bodily "washed" with pure water, according to the commandment (or word) of God (Eph. 5:25-27, Titus 3:5). In the NT context, such "washing" has no other legitimate meaning than one's baptism into Christ. For no other reason than one's baptism *into* Christ (Rom. 6:3) is one ever told to "wash" his body as a means of drawing near to God *through* Christ. While this washing alludes to what was required of the priests in preparation for them to minister to the tabernacle (Exod. 30:18-21, Lev. 16:4), here it has far higher significance.

---

access that before did not exist. There is also the idea here that this sacrifice remains forever "new," in that it never grows old, diminishes in power, or fades from memory. When we partake of the Lord's Supper, we do not remember an old, stale, or outdated offering; we honor an ever-present offering, one that is eternal, life-giving, and (thus) worthy of our remembrance.

149 JFB, *Commentary* (electronic), on 10:19.

The Levitical priests washed for physical and ritual purification; the believer is washed (immersed in water) to enter covenant with God, wherein he has access to the Father. Elsewhere, Peter explains that this washing/baptism is not for physical cleansing but a spiritual "appeal to God for a good conscience" (1 Peter 3:21). Thus, both the "inside…and the outside" (figurative of the conscience and body) of the believer are cleansed (see Mat. 23:26).

Our baptism into Christ is the physical demonstration of the "confession of our hope" (10:23). God's faithfulness to us ought to translate to our confidence and a living hope in Him. Our "confession" speaks to what we believe about God (who He is, what He has promised, and what He is able to perform) as well as our commitment to Him (who *we* are, what *we* have promised, and our *striving* to perform). God acts with divine grace, and we act in human faith: *both* actions are necessary for salvation. We are not to abandon or move away from this confession (1 Tim. 6:12-13): it is a binding vow made *to* God; it is a sacred covenant made *with* God. Therefore, one cannot forsake it without the severest of consequences (as the writer will shortly reveal). The statement, "He who promised is faithful," is offered as a test of the reader's sincerity: *He* is faithful to keep His promises to *you*; the question is, will *you* remain faithful in your promise to *Him*?

Stimulating One Another (10:24-25): Instead of doubting one's confession and contemplating one's abandonment of Christ, Christians are supposed to "consider [or, discover]" how to "stimulate" one another to be busy with the business of discipleship (10:24). "Stimulate" [Greek, *paroxusmos*] in this context means to provoke or prod someone (in a positive way) into doing what is right.[150] Those who focus on "love and good deeds" will get their minds off their internal self-doubts, troubles of this life, and even religious persecution. While we may not be persecuted today (yet), we still struggle against the assault of non-commitment, indifference, and apathy. The prescription for overcoming this remains the same: we are to stimulate others *and* be stimulated ourselves to demonstrate love and do good works. The "one another"-ness of this

---

150 Wuest, *Word Studies*, 182.

action, therefore, may have a twofold effect: we can be stimulated *through* our stimulation of others. Even if we receive nothing immediate from this ourselves, this is the visible behavior of God's people (Mat. 5:16, John 13:34-35); we are created "in Him" for this very purpose (Eph. 2:10).

"[N]ot forsaking our own assembling together..." (10:25).[151] While regularly assembling with sincere believers in public worship does not necessarily prevent one from drifting away, it is almost always true that one who "forsakes [or, abandons; deserts]" this assembling either will or has already begun to "waver." "Our author exhorts his readers to continue meeting together the more earnestly because he knows of some who were withdrawing from the Christian fellowship."[152]

This instruction goes far beyond a mere reference to church attendance. Those who disconnect themselves from the saints (either purposely or out of neglect) sever themselves from the source of teaching, mutual edification, and collective worship that are critical to their spiritual success. Paul (and other missionaries) established churches wherever they went for a reason: Christians need to mutually support one another to remain true to their "common faith" (Jude 1:3). Christians have a moral responsibility not only to keep their own faith alive but also to support the faith of other believers. Coming out of the world is difficult enough; *staying* out of the world over an extended period is even more difficult. Regular, positive, and collective reinforcement is crucial to overcome this difficulty. Even in the case of the Hebrew Christians, the struggle is enormous.

---

151 "The Greek word (the noun) is used nowhere else in the New Testament, except in 2 Thessalonians 2:1, where it is rendered *gathering together*. The verb is used in Matthew 23:3 Matthew 24:31, Mark 1:33, 13:27, Luke 12:1, 13:34, in all which places it is rendered *gathered together*. It properly means *an act of assembling*, or *a gathering together*, and is nowhere used in the New Testament in the sense of an assembly, or the church. The command, then, here is, *to meet together* for the worship of God, and it is enjoined on Christians as an important duty to do it" (Barnes, *Notes*, 234; all emphases are his).

152 Bruce, *Commentary*, 253.

> The aim of the whole epistle is to counteract the defection
> from Christianity which had set in among the Jewish Christian
> readers. They had begun to revert to Judaism, to think the Jewish
> priesthood, Temple, sacrifices, etc., [was] the real thing, to turn
> from this crucified Christ, etc. We see here that "some" were
> giving up their fellowship with the church. We conclude that
> they were going back to the Jewish synagogues...in order to be
> Jews again.[153]

Various interpretations have been offered for the "day drawing near" phrase (10:25). Some believe it is the Second Coming; others, the first day of the week (Sunday); still others, the destruction of Jerusalem (in AD 70). In the context of this epistle, all of these seem to apply at once. However, the antecedent (i.e., prior subjective point of reference) is "assembling together." Thus, it seems logical and natural to conclude that the "day" refers to the day in which "assembling together" is to take place. To impose either the Second Coming or the destruction of Jerusalem here—even though both may apply in view of a *larger* context—is to force too much into the text without substantiation.

A Most Serious Warning (10:26-31): The writer of *Hebrews* has thus far used sound reasoning, gentle persuasion, and appeals to the sacred Scripture to convince his readers not to turn away from their commitment to Christ. Now he uses blunt and even terrifying language (10:26-31). Believers need to know in no uncertain terms that defaulting on one's faith in Christ is a grievous sin and puts one's soul in terrible jeopardy—even if one claims to serve God through a different means (e.g., through the Law of Moses, or even a "spiritual but not religious" belief). "Preachers think it wise not to appeal to the motive of fear. But by not frightening men into heaven they fail to frighten them away from hell."[154]

In the Greek text, "willfully [or, deliberately]" is the first word in the sentence (of 10:26), and accordingly demands the greatest emphasis.

---

153 Lenski, *Interpretation*, 354.
154 Lenski, *Interpretation*, 362.

Thus, the following words do not describe one who has never been a Christian, or a Christian who continues to *struggle* against sin (as we all do, and not always successfully). It describes a Christian who *willfully* sins (without repentance) by abandoning altogether his commitment to Christ.

We might understand this passage (10:26) to mean: if a person will not repent of his "willful" sin, then he will face judgment when he dies. We would do well to read the passage (and its companion passage, 6:4-8) more closely. The writer speaks of one's state of existence *even while he lives*: he has no more *opportunity* for a "sacrifice for sins." Sacrifice for sin is not something that benefits a person when he is dead but only while he lives. One who abandons his faith in Christ risks the forfeiture of any further recourse (or atonement) for his sinful state. He has nothing else to look forward to except God's vengeful judgment (10:27). In other words, this passage teaches that a person may reach a point of no return which no penitence can reverse, and for which no prayers can intercede (see 1 John 5:16).

If this is true, the question remains: who *determines* when a person has reached the "point of no return"? Certainly, it is not us: people cannot speak with any authority on this. The final decision lies with God Himself, for only He can absolutely know a person's heart and only He can know when that final line has been crossed. But the warning is grave and intentionally intimidating: *do not toy lightly with Him who has the power to destroy your soul for your irreverence* (see Luke 12:5). "Fire" (10:27) is symbolic of God's judgment against His enemies (which is the context of Isa. 26:11; see 2 Thess. 1:7-8).

To underscore his point, the writer (again) draws upon Israel's own history (10:28-29). If an Israelite died "without mercy" (i.e., without restraint or pity) for sinning against the Law of Moses[155]—a mere shadow of good things to come—then how much stronger will be the

---

[155] "two or three witnesses"—not necessarily *eyewitnesses* but those who are capable and competent to serve as a kind of grand jury—are sufficient to evaluate and render a verdict concerning a particular case; see Deut. 17:6-7 and 19:15.

punishment for sinning against the gospel of Christ? (Recall comments on 2:1-4.) This person has forsaken every appeal for divine intercession; he has turned his back on God's finest divine gifts. Through his "willful" sin (10:29) he:

- ❑ **tramples underfoot the Son of God.** This is not a mere rejection of Christ, but one accompanied with contempt. Christ went to great lengths to prove His divinity, even to the point of raising Himself from the dead. One who turns away from Him—especially after having once *believed* in His testimony—brings upon himself an awful curse. The willful sinner implies that God is a liar since He endorsed Jesus as His Son (but now he does not believe this—or does not care).
- ❑ **regards the "blood of the covenant" as unclean.** He shows no appreciation for the blood to which he once appealed for the forgiveness of his sins. He thus shows no regard for the *life* Christ led to make His blood worthy or the *death* Christ died to shed that blood. Though he once made a binding covenant with God, the sinner now breaks that covenant purposely and without justification. The "blood of the covenant" is the life-giving agent that ratifies or makes active the covenant between God and the one in need of salvation.
- ❑ **has insulted the Spirit of grace.** To deny the blood of the crucified Christ is to deny the One who has revealed Him through the miracle of revelation and the testimony of miracles themselves.[156] As it is impossible to separate God's Spirit from God Himself, this is tantamount to an insult to the Father. There appears a direct connection between this passage and the unpardonable sin of denying the (testimony of) the Holy Spirit (see Mat. 12:22-37).

"For we know Him" (10:30)—i.e., you Jews already know who God is and what He is capable of. The quotes are from Deut. 32:35-36, 41 and are part of the Song of Moses which was regularly sung as part of

---

156 See Zech. 12:10, the only other time "Spirit of grace" is used in Scripture. In that context, God promised His "Spirit of grace" to His people so that they would recognize the One who was "pierced" for them.

Jewish synagogue worship. This song characterized God as One who will not let His enemies escape their due punishment, regardless of how long it appears to take to bring it about (see 2 Peter 3:3-9 as a parallel thought). Divine vengeance (or retribution, as in 2 Thess. 1:8) is not only something God *will* carry out; because of His absolute moral responsibility to righteousness, it is something He *must* carry out. He cannot overlook any violation of or insult toward His divine nature or holy character. Salvation and judgment come from the same God: the One who rescues the penitent from prison also puts into prison forever sinners who refuse to repent.

Anyone who resists salvation through the Son of God becomes an enemy of God, no matter how pious or righteous he believes himself to be (Mat. 12:30, John 14:6). To "fall into the hands of the living God" (10:31) can be something good and merciful, as in 2 Sam. 24:14. But in the present case, it clearly refers to an unspeakably dreadful and terrifying experience. The implication is that such a person has no recourse, no further opportunity for repentance, and no means of escaping the wrath of God (John 3:36).

The Need for Endurance (10:32-39): The writer has spoken as forcefully toward the Hebrew Christians because it was necessary. Now (as in 6:10), he softens his tone considerably to acknowledge how these Christians had previously shown their great faith in times past—the "former days" (10:32). The "great conflict of sufferings" may allude to literal historical persecutions from unconverted Jews and/or the Roman Emperor Nero (reigned AD 54-68).[157] Having received Christian baptism, these Jews were excommunicated from the Jewish community; having pledged allegiance to Christ as Lord, they were charged by Rome with treason against the emperor. Even if they themselves had not faced persecution directly, they stood by (and identified with) those who had.

---

[157] "Conflict" here is from the Greek word *athlesis*, from which we get the English word "athletic," which implies a contest, challenge, or struggle (Strong, *Dictionary*, G119). "By casting the readers' situation in athletic imagery, the author is able to portray them as victors (cf. 12:1ff), which contributes to the positive encouragement" (McClister, *Commentary*, 369).

"Prisoners" here (10:33-34, as in Mat. 25:36 and Heb. 13:3) does not refer to people imprisoned for ungodly crimes, but brethren imprisoned for their *faith in Christ*. Previously, the Hebrew Christians "joyfully" accepted these hardships, despite the losses (of property, reputation, civil rights, and human dignity) which they incurred (10:34). They looked ahead to what lay beyond this life for their compensation for losses and reward for faithfulness (see Heb. 11:13-16). Nonetheless, even though their lives had been spared (see Heb. 12:4), they had grown *disillusioned* with the source of their confidence through these protracted difficulties. Battle-weariness had set in: while having survived the conflict itself, they are now struggling with the despondency and doubts created *by* the conflict.

The writer (in 10:35-39) makes a tacit allusion to the soldier who, amid the battle, lost his morale, threw aside his shield and sword, turned his back on the enemy, and ran for his life. Such is an act of lost confidence as well as self-preservation. In ancient times, this was considered an extremely shameful act; those who carried it out were often humiliated later and shunned by society, if not outright executed.[158] One's *confidence* in the Rewarder is necessary if he is to receive the great reward for his own efforts—in this case, his unwavering faith (10:35; see Luke 21:19 and Heb. 11:6).[159] Endurance will not exist without confidence; the one who refuses to endure also forfeits his reward.

"For you have need of endurance..." (10:36)—a blunt but necessary admonition. Perseverance and endurance are similar but not identical. Perseverance means to go through [*per-*] some trial of severity [*-severe*]. Endurance, however, is seeing something what you started to its appropriate end—i.e., the full duration of the task. While both

---

158 Milligan, *Commentary*, 291.

159 "Confidence" here is from the Greek word *parresia*, which is often used with reference to the boldness of one's speech and outspoken public admission (Strong, *Dictionary* [electronic], G3954; Vincent, *Word Studies* [electronic], on 10:35). Thus, the Hebrews' confidence was not merely a loss of heart within; it was also a lack of proclamation without—i.e., a refusal to publicly defend Christ and His gospel as *God's truth*. Christ will not reward anyone who refuses to defend Him before men—for any reason (Mat. 10:32-33).

virtues are necessary (and both English words are often translated from the same Greek word [*hupomone*]), it is the idea of "endurance" that the *Hebrews* writer means here. The Hebrew Christians had already persevered in several former trials, but they have not yet finished what they started. The "will of God" is what they promised to uphold, regardless of the difficulty or cost. One who will not conform to the will of the Father certainly will not receive what the Father promised (Mat. 7:21-23). The *promise*, then, is conditional; it is contingent upon continued faithfulness.

In time, the writer reminds his readers, "He who is coming will come" (10:37-38). Specifically, this may refer to:

- a private judgment against these Christians themselves, as in the case of Jesus' warnings of this against the churches of Asia (Rev. 2 – 3).
- Jesus' predicted judgment against the Jewish nation (Mat. 24:27-31).
- the Second Coming of Christ, as already mentioned in 9:28.

In a real sense, all these references fit the context of this passage, and all necessitate the same things: faithfulness, preparedness, confidence, endurance, holding fast to one's confession, etc. The quote here from Hab. 2:3-4 has been re-worded from the Septuagint (the Greek translation of the OT) to bring out the intended emphasis. Paul used this passage to emphasize justification by faith (Rom. 1:17); here, however, the emphasis is on God's great displeasure with those who "shrink back" from Him. Just as God (in Habakkuk's day) would neither save godless Chaldeans (a.k.a. Babylonians) who attacked Israel *nor* the faithless Israelites who were under this attack, so He will not save faithless Christians who abandon their confidence in His Son. "Delay, from the human standpoint, is not delay at all from the viewpoint of God. His will is certain of accomplishment."[160]

"But we are not of those who shrink back…" (10:39)—i.e., the writer gives all benefit of doubt to his readers that they will not succumb to the temptation to forfeit their reward. Furthermore, abandonment of one's

---

160 Coffman, *Commentary*, 248.

faith is simply not consistent with those who claim to be God's people. Faith is never about shrinking back (or retreating) but always about moving forward (or advancing). God never teaches us to pull backward in faith but only to reach forward to what lies ahead (Phil. 3:13).

This all-important subject of *faith*, having been introduced again (recall 4:2 and 6:12), will take center stage as the writer takes time to commend those who *have* confidently endured through faith (chapter 11).

Faith and Those Who Have Exemplified It (11:1–40)

Nowhere else in the NT is the subject of faith so clearly expounded upon than in the eleventh chapter of *Hebrews*. While Paul emphasized the *requirement* of faith in the process of justification in *Romans*, the *Hebrews* writer speaks of the continued *implementation* of faith in those who have been justified. While the word has not been used much in this epistle prior to now, "faith"—or the lack of it—is the core issue of those to whom the writer has addressed.[161] In the most basic sense, "faith" is "*a positive response to God*" which "involves the heart, the mind, the will, the emotions, obedience, commitment, loyalty, etc. It is a generic term that covers the entire 'package' of things that comprise a positive response to God and his word."[162]

While believers are to "walk by faith, not by sight" (2 Cor. 5:7), the recipients of this letter were "walking" by what they *saw*, not according to the way things really *were*. In their eyes, Christianity had run its course, was failing, or simply was not what they thought it would be. They concluded that Judaism must be superior to Christianity, since they were considering a return to it; in doing so, they would be

---

[161] For prior usages, see Heb. 2:17, 3:2, and 3:6 in reference to *Christ's* faithfulness to God. The only other direct references: Moses being described as "faithful in all [God's] house as a servant (3:5); and ancient Israel being found *not* faithful to God despite the "good news" they were given (4:2).

[162] McLister, *Commentary*, 381; emphases are his.

abandoning their faith in what had been promised to them in Christ.[163] It was necessary, then, to speak of the faith that God required of them, if indeed they were to remain in favor with Him. Faith is, by necessary implication (11:1-2):

- **"assurance [or, substance] of things hoped for [or, expected]."** Hope requires a credible *reason to exist*; faith in God requires a *reason to believe* Him. God cannot expect anyone to "hope" in Him if He has not provided this reason. But once He *has* provided it (and He has—see John 20:30-31 and Acts 17:30-31), then every person has a credible, factual, and confident basis for his belief; he can become a believer.
- **"conviction [or, evidence] of things not seen."** This speaks to the certainty of what cannot be known by (mere) human observation. God exists—of this we may be certain—but we cannot *prove* this statement with direct, fully conclusive evidence, for none of us has *seen* Him (1 John 4:12). But invisible truths are still truths; even the physical world operates on invisible laws, principles, and forces. To deny God's existence only because He is invisible to human sight is irrational, especially since He is spiritual in nature (John 1:18, 4:24). "Things not seen" not only refers to things invisible to the human eye but also things that have not yet happened (but have been foretold).[164]
- **how we, just like "men of old," gain approval.**[165] Since "the righteous man shall live by faith" (Hab. 2:4, Romans 1:17), this requires a higher authority than man himself to provide a standard

---

163 Judaism had been around for some 1,500 years, while Christianity had existed for less than 40 years. One might argue that Judaism had *proved* to be far more enduring than Christianity; therefore, a return to Judaism was understandable. However, this fails to consider all the arguments made thus far, as well as Jesus' predictions that the Jewish system was about to be permanently terminated.

164 For a comparable passage, see 2 Peter 3:3-9, where "mockers" based their entire conclusions upon what they were able to see, not on what had been promised (by a God who had already fulfilled every promised He had ever made to date).

165 "Men of old" is from the same Greek word (*presbuteros*) from which we get "elders" (as in 1 Tim. 5:17 and 1 Peter 5:1). It likely refers here to "the fathers" in 1:1—those through whom God spoke in ancient times.

of this righteousness. People do not define what "faith" is but God alone does. To *have* faith is a human decision, but it is *God's* decision as to whether this agrees with His standard of faith. Just as God has always approved of those who base their faith in Him, so He continues to do this today.

"By faith" is an expression of high commendation to those who exemplify it (11:3). Faith is God's measure of one's trust in Him, even though the believer has not yet *received* what was hoped for or *seen* the One who guarantees it. The writer here begins with a very general example of this: one who believes that "the word of God" created the world exhibits *faith* in God and His supernatural activity (Gen. 1:1-3, John 1:1-3, 2 Peter 3:5, etc.). The visible was created by the invisible; a supernatural Being created the natural world. Such conclusions are based on what is not humanly observable or reproducible. The only way one can accept God's explanation of "what happened" is *by faith*: there is no alternative. This does not mean one must exercise *blind* faith, for God has provided sufficient evidence of what He has done and requires men to believe rather than see (Rom. 1:18-20, John 20:29).[166] Faith that is blind has no evidence, testimony, or reason to believe, and God does *not* approve of such "faith." The "men of old"—i.e., the ancients who lived by faith in God—"gained approval [or, obtained a good testimony]" because of their faith in the Creator of the world.

At this point (11:4ff), the writer provides numerous and specific examples from Scripture of those who have indeed lived "by faith."[167]

---

166 The popular argument against Creation usually boils down to this: there is no science to support it. Ironically, there is no science to support the Big Bang Theory, the Theory of Evolution, or the Theory of Everything, but this does not stop intelligent people from believing in these. Faith in God is predicated on physical, moral, and eyewitness evidence (including the written record of Scripture), not scientists. Even though Creation preceded science, the laws of physics and energy are natural expectations of an all-powerful and all-intelligent God who alone could design them.

167 Some commentators point out that Adam and Eve are conspicuously missing from this "roll call of the faithful." Adam Clarke remarked, "Adam's rebellion against his Maker was too great and too glaring to permit his name ever to be mentioned with honor or respect" (*Clarke's Commentary*, vol. VI [New York: Abingdon-Cokebury Press [no date], 762). But is this the real and final reason? We will have to accept the fact that

This is helpful to us because we might not at first consider some of the following actions as demonstrations of *faith* but simply of individual *choices*. But the two things do in fact work together: faith *is* a choice. One must choose to be faithful; it is not something forced upon him. Powerful as He is, God cannot *make* a person be faithful to Him. Likewise, for a person to refuse to have faith is also a choice. Powerful as He is, God cannot *make* a person be unfaithful to Him.

Abel Lived by Faith (11:4): The first personal example offered is that of Abel, Adam and Eve's second son (11:4; see Gen. 4:1-5). Abel's offering of a blood sacrifice was superior to his brother Cain's vegetable sacrifice; more than this, Abel's attitude demonstrated faith in his compliance to what God expected, while Cain's demonstrated something evil (11:4; see Gen. 4:4 and 1 John 3:11-12).[168] God "testified" or approved of Abel's offering by accepting it; in accepting Abel's sacrifice, God also accepted or approved of Abel himself. Abel's blood "still speaks," that is, it continues to offer an illustration to *us* of what "approved" faith looks like. (Soon, in 12:24, the writer will say that Christ's blood "speaks" far better than Abel's.) There is another consideration as well: "The blood of Abel warns the murderer, and every wrong-doer, that the Creator will yet require that the accounts be settled"—that a day of final reckoning is sure to come.[169]

Enoch Lived by Faith (11:5): The next example offered is of Enoch, the son of Jared and the father of Methuselah, of the seventh generation of Adam through his son Seth (11:5; see Gen. 5:18-24). Everyone else in the Gen. 5 genealogy "died," but Enoch did not see death and thus avoided both the curse against Adam (Gen. 3:19) and the curse of the

---

the Holy Spirit allowed the omissions and inclusions in this "roll call" as He saw fit, for there is no objective answer otherwise.

168   The implication in the Gen. 4 account is that blood sacrifice was not only required as part of God's covenantal relationship with His people but had also been instructed in some manner. Neither Cain nor Abel was acting on his own in providing these offerings; each man was responding to a command that has not been recorded for us. This command had to have had specific requirements for God to have approved of one offering but rejected the other.

169   Coffman, *Commentary*, 255.

Flood (Gen. 6).[170] There is little that is known of Enoch, except that (it appears) he was a preacher of righteousness amid a human population that was growing increasingly hostile to God (compare Gen. 6:6 and Jude 1:14-15). Because of his faithfulness—which, by implication, must have been significant—God "took" him from the earth without having to experience human death. Obviously, God never would have spared Enoch of the curse of death or the curse of the Flood unless he had found favor with Him because of his faith.

Faith Is Essential for Pleasing God (11:6): The writer wants his readers to dwell upon this thought for a moment: *no one* can find favor with God apart from having faith in Him (11:6). It is not just unlikely but "impossible" to please God without putting faith in Him, which means believing that He exists; obeying His commandments; and trusting in His ability to perform in ways that exceed human ability or comprehension. Having faith in God is equivalent to being a seeker of God: one who does not actively seek Him (in the way He approves) also has no faith in Him, regardless of his claims. God's majesty, supremacy, and sovereign authority warrant our pursuit of Him. Because He is greater than us and superior to everything that exists in the world, people *ought* to be seeking Him. (It is very sad when people give greater attention—time, expense, and eagerness—to the pursuit of ghosts, "blind forces of nature," and extra-terrestrial life than to the Creator of the world and Source of our existence.) And those who do seek Him believe that they will be rewarded for their pursuit.

Noah Lived by Faith (11:7): The writer's next example of one who lived "by faith" is Noah (whose name means "rest"), the great-grandson of Enoch (Gen. 5:28-29). Noah had never seen a "flood upon the earth" before *the* Flood, nor had he ever seen a massive ark prior to the one which God commissioned him to build (Gen. 6:5-12). He acted in faith, having an assurance that God would do what He said (both in

---

170 In the future, there will be many others besides Enoch and Elijah who will not see death. All the faithful who are alive at the coming of Christ will be "changed" and translated into heaven without having to die (1 Cor. 15:50-53). Very likely, this is what Jesus spoke of in John 11:26.

His judgment against the world *and* His preservation of Noah and his family) *and* a conviction in what he had never seen (Luke 17:26-27). He also acted "in reverence," that is, in holy fear of a God powerful enough to condemn in judgment *and* save through providence (2 Peter 2:5). Fittingly, he is the first man in Scripture to be identified as "righteous."

Abraham Lived by Faith (11:8-18): Abraham, one of the greatest heroes of Israel, exhibited unprecedented faith as far as the biblical record is concerned. For this reason, he is referred to as the father of the faithful, having produced many "sons" of faith (Gal. 3:6-9, 29). When God told Abraham to do something, *by faith in God* he did it. The first thing God had Abraham do was to *separate himself* from his father's (Terah's) family so that, in essence, God could be his new Father (Gen. 12:1-9). Thus, Abraham left the city-state of Ur in ancient Babylonia and became a nomadic tent-dweller in a foreign land. In other words, he left a man-made city to find a "city...whose architect and builder is God" (11:10).

While it appears from some translations that Sarah is suddenly mentioned on par with Abraham (11:11), the original Greek text's grammatical construction does not support this.[171] It is Abraham's faith which is and remains the specific focus here. This is not to say that Sarah had no faith, but she did not have the power to conceive apart from Abraham's own faithfulness,[172] and Abraham is the one to whom God made the promise. Thus, even though his hope in human ability (to produce an heir through Sarah) was dead (i.e., due to the human impossibility of it being realized), Abraham's hope in God was very much alive (see Gen. 17:15-22, 18:1-15, and Rom. 4:16-22). We see a progressive narrowing of ideas and context in this entire passage, from

---

171 JFB's *Commentary* (electronic) on 11:11, for example, says: "God empowered Sarah, overcoming her doubt (Genesis 18:12) and infusing her with faith." This is not a natural conclusion of either the Genesis account or the text in *Hebrews*. God does not "infuse" a person with faith but gives him (or her) a sufficient reason to believe and then leaves it to that person to either act upon that reason or not.

172 The margin reference for 11:11 in NASB reads, "Lit., power for the laying down of seed," which demonstrates the power of the male and not the female—thus, the faith of Abraham, not Sarah (Kistemaker, *NTC*, 323).

general to specific: a *place*, a *land*, a *city*, a *child* (of promise).

But Abraham never saw the *entire fulfillment* of the promise (of a great nation), since he died before it happened. The writer takes this opportunity to expound on that thought for a moment: *so it is for all of us* (11:13-16). All who walk by faith in God are "strangers and exiles [or, aliens]" on this earth (1 Peter 2:11). No one realizes *all* the promises of God in his own lifetime or this earthly context. The "country" and "city" God has prepared for the faithful lies beyond the scope of human grasp or vision (John 14:2-3, 2 Cor. 4:18, Phil. 3:20-21, and 2 Peter 3:13). "God is not ashamed to be called their God" alludes again to the "I will be their God, and they will be My people" statement that resonates throughout Scripture (recall 8:10).

Having said these things, the writer now returns to the account of Abraham (11:17-18). The greatest test of Abraham's faith was his decision to give up Isaac, his son of divine promise, in obedience to God's request (Gen. 22:1-10). God designated Isaac as the critical link to all that lay in Abraham's future; without Isaac, there would be no national greatness or future blessings to "all the families of the earth" (Gen. 12:1-3). Abraham did not know how God was going to rectify the problem that Isaac's death would create, but he believed that God *would* rectify it, even if it meant that He would raise his son from the dead. If God can give life to a dead womb and a dead hope, it seemed reasonable to Abraham to believe that God could give life to a dead person. As it turned out, even the *sparing* of Isaac's life serves as a kind of resurrection parable, since he was (in essence) condemned to death but given a new life instead.

Isaac, Jacob, and Joseph Lived by Faith (11:20-22): While Isaac never had to face the difficult testing his father endured, he still lived in faith, believing in the divine promise that directly involved himself and his sons (Gen. 27). Having transmitted this blessing to his son Jacob—whom he was deceived into believing was his son Esau— Isaac manifested faith that God's providence toward his family would continue even after his death. His son Jacob also lived with the belief that he was an active participant in God's divine plan (compare Gen. 28:3-4 and 48:4). He knew that, even after his death, the promise would continue through Joseph's sons, Ephraim and Manasseh, who serve (in this passage) as representatives of all the sons of Israel. (Since Joseph had become a "son" to Pharaoh, Jacob gave to his grandson Joseph's inheritance.) As for Joseph, he saw the future of his family beyond the borders of Egypt since he asked that, when they finally did leave, they would take his bones with them (Gen. 50:24-25, Exod. 13:19, and Josh. 24:32).

Moses Lived by Faith (11:23-28): The next great hero of Scripture after Joseph is unquestionably Moses. Yet, the writer begins this account with the faith of Moses' parents (11:23), Amram and Jochebed (Exod. 6:20). Pharaoh, to keep the Hebrews from revolting against him, ordered that all the male babies be put to death (Exodus 1:16, 22). Amram and Jochebed, however, hid Moses for three months, then put him in a basket in the Nile River, hoping that he would be delivered through some other means.[173]

God *did* preserve Moses through the compassion of Pharaoh's own daughter (Exod. 2:1-10). But when Moses grew up, he exhibited his own personal faith in Jehovah rather than the polytheism of Egypt. Though educated in Egyptian language, culture, and society (Acts 7:21-22), he continued to identify with the Hebrew people. Joseph had become a "son" to Pharaoh out of necessity; however, Moses refused to remain as Pharaoh's son (i.e., of his household), sensing that the time of Israel's deliverance was near. The idea of Moses choosing the "reproach of Christ" (11:25) over the riches of Egypt makes it sound as if Moses had personal knowledge of Jesus. This, of course, is said in hindsight, but incorporates Christ's spiritual deliverance of His people with God's deliverance of Israel and its patriarchs (compare 1 Cor. 10:4). According to Stephen's account (Acts 7:24-29), we know that Moses presupposed

---

173 In a sense, they *did* comply with the decree—they put their son in the Nile River—but not with the intention that Pharaoh had implied. Pharaoh's decree called for the Hebrew boys' destruction by drowning; Moses' parents sought the preservation of their son's life.

some facts about this deliverance, yet after killing an Egyptian he was forced to leave Egypt. Even so, he never abandoned his faith in Jehovah.

Forty years later, God appointed Moses to lead His people out of Egypt accompanied by great demonstrations of His power. Moses was instructed to keep the Passover observance, even though the tenth plague (death of the firstborn of Egypt) was unprecedented and difficult even to imagine (11:28; see Exod. 12). The same can be said of the parting of the Red Sea: this was unprecedented and impossible by any human effort. But Moses believed the Lord and acted in faith, and Israel walked a dry path through the middle of the waters as a result (11:29; see Exod. 14). Through this one miraculous event, God not only saved Israel but also destroyed the strength of Egypt.

Joshua Lived by Faith (11:30): While the writer does not mention Joshua by name in this next example, he certainly is implied (11:30). It was he before whom the "angel of the LORD" appeared with instructions concerning how to defeat Jericho (Josh. 5:13 – 6:5). Joshua was faithful to keep God's commandment concerning this, even though what he was asked to do was unprecedented and defied any natural explanation. We also cannot ignore the faith of all those who marched *with* Joshua around that city—the Israelite army as well as the priests.

Rahab Acted by Faith (11:31): Rahab, though a prostitute and a Canaanite—and therefore under a divine curse—played an impressive role in the unfolding plan of God (11:31). Not only is she one of the few women in the OT mentioned for her faith (see Josh. 2 and 6), she also is included in the genealogy of Christ (Mat. 1:5). As Joshua's men spied out the city of Jericho, she believed in God and what He was planning to do and sought redemption for her and her family. For her courage and faith, she is honored here (and in James 2:25).

Other Men and Women Who Lived by Faith (11:32-38): The next group of examples of faith (11:32) is not in chronological order, nor is this necessary. It appears that the writer may simply be recalling these Bible figures from memory. Certainly, some of these men had serious character flaws—think of Samson, for example—and yet they are honored here not because they were flawless, but for the *faith* they exhibited.

- **Gideon** [a.k.a. Jerub-baal], with only 300 men, overwhelmed a Midianite army that seemed innumerable and invincible (Judg. 6 – 8).
- **Barak** fought successfully against the Canaanites, trusting in divine counsel through the prophetess Deborah (Judg. 4 – 5). (While Deborah's role goes unmentioned here, it is necessarily implied. The Hebrew readers would certainly know this.)
- **Samson** repeatedly fought against the Philistines, and especially sought justice against them for gouging out his eyes—a retribution which cost him his own life (Judg. 13 – 16). Even though Samson's reasons for acting were not always virtuous, he believed that God's power was the source of his own strength. "It was not [the writer's] purpose to commend all that was done by even the best and most illustrious of these men of faith. Abraham sinned, and so did Moses, although their example was far more elevated than that of Samson. But when the Spirit of the Lord came upon him, he performed some feats, in the exercise of faith, which are without a parallel in human history."[174]
- **Jephthah** fought successfully against the Ammonites and punished the arrogance of Ephraim (Judg. 11 – 12). Jephthah did not always appear to be a model of virtuous character, but he did manifest great faith in God—even to his own hurt.
- **David**, successor to King Saul and the father of Solomon, was the most prominent and one of the most faithful of all the Israelite kings. During his reign he enlarged Israel's borders, defeated all his enemies, and established a kingdom that God has continued even to this day (in Christ—Luke 1:31-33). He was not only Israel's great king but also served as a spiritual leader and foreshadow of an even greater Messiah. He was also a prophet in his own right since many of David's psalms contain messianic prophecies.

---

174 Milligan, *Commentary*, 325.

- **Samuel and the prophets:** Samuel (1 Sam. 2:18ff) is considered the head of a long line of prophets among Israel (Acts 3:24). Previously, Israel's leaders were often judges; Samuel served as both judge *and* prophet (Acts 13:20). "The prophets" includes not only those whose oracles or books remain today as part of the Hebrew Bible, but also those mentioned within OT history (such as Nathan, Elijah, Elisha, Micaiah, etc.).

Now the writer turns his attention from specific names to specific acts that were *accomplished* through faith (11:33-35a). For example, the faithful:

- **conquered kingdoms:** think of men like Joshua and David.
- **performed {acts of} righteousness** [or, administered (or enforced) justice]: think of the judges, Samuel, David, Solomon, Josiah, and several other righteous kings.
- **obtained promises:** think of Abraham, Isaac, Jacob, Joseph, Joshua (Josh. 23:14), Hannah, David, and many others.
- **shut the mouths of lions:** think of Daniel (Dan. 6), but also consider Samson and David, who both single-handedly killed lions (Judg. 14:6, 1 Sam. 17:34-37).
- **quenched the power** [or, fury] **of fire:** think of Daniel's friends Shadrach, Meshach, and Abednego (Dan. 3).
- **escaped the edge of the sword:** think specifically of David (numerous times), Elijah (from Jezebel—1 Kings 19:8-10) and Elisha (2 Kings 6:31-32), even though many unrecorded accounts could satisfy this description, including the extra-biblical history of Mattathias and his sons (a.k.a. the Maccabees).
- **despite personal weakness became strong:** think of Samson, David (despite Bathsheba and other downfalls), and the post-exilic Jews who, despite the humility of captivity, overcame great obstacles and difficulties. We should not forget NT examples as well, especially that of Paul (2 Cor. 12:10) and several of his fellow workers.
- **became mighty in war:** think of Joshua, Caleb, several of the judges, Saul, David, and several more of the kings of Israel and Judah.

- **put foreign armies to flight:** think of Gideon, David (especially regarding the Philistines, after the defeat of Goliath), and several other kings of Israel and Judah.
- **women received back…resurrection:** think of the women who sheltered Elijah (1 Kings 17:24) and Elisha (2 Kings 4:8-37), whose sons were raised from the dead as a direct result of their faith in God and His prophets.

Having offered examples of great acts of faith, the writer now turns his attention to what men and women have *suffered* because of their faith (11:35b-38). For example, the faithful have endured:

- **torture:** there are no specific OT examples of actual torture, except in the apocrypha (2 Maccabees 6). Literally, the Greek word refers to the beating of a drum, thus "to torture by beating, to beat to death."[175] However, "torture" can have different meanings than just external, physical affliction (consider Lot, for example—2 Peter 2:7-8). The point is: men and women suffered for their faith in various ways, not willing to let go of their faith in God even under great duress or threat of martyrdom. While the concept of "resurrection" was shrouded in types and foreshadows in the OT, it was generally understood that Israelites who died in faith would be reunited in a future regeneration of Israel (see John 11:24 and Mat. 19:28). This passage (11:35) alludes to a basic understanding that the loss of one's life here would lead to the gain of a better life in the hereafter—thus, a "better resurrection" than simply prolonging one's typical earthly existence.
- **mockings [or, jeers], scourgings [or, floggings], chains, imprisonment:** think of Jeremiah (Jer. 20:2), Micaiah (1 Kings 22:27), John the Baptist (Mat. 14:3), Jesus, the apostles, Paul, Silas, and no doubt many others. Most of the OT prophets faced ridicule, and sometimes physical abuse, for their roles as God's spokesmen;

---

175 W. E. Vines, *Vine's Expository Dictionary of New Testament Words* (STBC; no date), 4:145. Lenski writes: "The verb means to stretch upon a wheel-like frame, the body becoming taut like a drum, which is then beaten until the victim yields or slowly dies in agony. In IV Macc. 5:32 the instrument used for this torture is…'wheel'" (*Interpretation*, 418).

several of the NT preachers did not fare any better.
- **stoning:** think of Naboth (1 Kings 21:10-15), Zechariah,[176] Stephen, Paul, and no doubt many others. Stoning was a common method of execution among the Jews (see Mat. 21:35).
- **being sawn in two:** according to Jewish tradition, the prophet Isaiah was put into a hollow log (or between two boards) which was then sawn in two.[177] Other than this, no other specific incident is known to us, but actual incidents may have been known to the Hebrews writer (based upon 2 Sam. 12:31 and 1 Chron. 20:3).
- **temptation:** think of Joseph (with Potiphar's wife) or Moses (with the treasures of Egypt). Consider also every man and woman who at some time or another has had to decide between the seduction of the world and obedience to God—and chose obedience. More specifically, consider every instance where a servant of God has been faced with death because of his faith, and was tempted to recant his faith in order spare his life (but did not).
- **death by the sword:**[178] think of the many prophets who were killed in Elijah's day during Jezebel's campaign to eliminate them (1 Kings 19:10). Think also of the priests whom Saul slaughtered (1 Sam. 22:19), Uriah the prophet (Jer. 26:20-23), John the Baptist, James (Acts 12:1-2), Paul (according to tradition), and no doubt many others.
- **going about in sheepskins, goatskins, etc.:** think of Elijah and John the Baptist, but likely many others also fit this description. The implication here is that of humility, destitution, and severe hardship. The writer presents an interesting perspective here: "men of whom the world was not worthy"—i.e., this is just the opposite of how the *world* thought of them (as in Acts 22:22). It is the unbelieving world that is not worthy of these faithful men, not the other way around.

---

176 Not the Zechariah who authored the book by this name but a different prophet (2 Chron. 24:21-22).

177 Kistemaker, *NTC*, 355, fn. 69.

178 Lit., "died by sword-slaughter," implying a mass-execution rather than an individual one (Wuest, *Word Studies*, 210); yet either of these meanings would support the writer's intention.

- **wandering in deserts, mountains, caves, and holes in the ground:** think of David and his men (1 Sam. 24:1), Elijah (1 Kings 19:4), Obadiah and the prophets (1 Kings 18:4, 13), John the Baptist (Mat. 3:1-4), and undoubtedly many others, including Jesus Himself (Luke 9:58).

Approved by Their Faith (11:39-40): In the beginning of this discourse (recall 11:2), the writer declared, "For by it [faith] the men of old gained approval." Even so, such men did not receive *in this life* the entirety of what had been promised them (11:39-40). They believed in God's promise without having seen God, the future, or their own salvation (recall 11:1). They also believed that the promise was worth more than what this world could give them, and that believing in God was far superior to believing in anything or anyone else. In many cases, they put their lives on the line—or even forfeited their lives altogether—based on this belief. The *full* promise, which takes in the big picture perspective, included:

- "all the families of the earth will be blessed" (Gen. 12:3).
- fulfillment of all prophecies concerning God's people of covenant (Israel).
- realization (or manifestation) of the kingdom of God (under Christ's kingship).
- the coming of Messiah and His universal redemption.
- ultimate judgment of the world: final vindication of the faithful *and* final destruction of their enemies (as graphically depicted in 2 Thess. 1:6-9).
- each faithful believer's personal reward: eternal fellowship with the Father.

The fact that these promises were (or are) yet to be fulfilled does not reflect poorly on God's *ability* to fulfill them, but simply indicates that the great saga of humankind has not yet run its full course. The subject here is *faith*: it takes great faith to believe confidently that all that has been *promised* will be *fulfilled* in due time, and not necessarily in one's own lifetime.

At the same time, we have far more than these "men of old" ever had because of Christ and the gospel message revealed from heaven. Christ has not only fulfilled the signs and types known to the ancients, He provides irrefutable support for all that *we also* have been promised (Acts 17:30-31, Eph. 1:13-14). He is our "something better," having provided us a better covenant and better promises (recall 8:6). Thus, the ancients were not "made perfect" *before* or *instead* of us (Christians) but *with* us (recall 9:15). The faithful of any era are "made perfect" through the offering of Christ (Rom. 3:23-25).[179]

The Need for Focus and Discipline (12:1-17)

Fixing Our Eyes on Jesus (12:1-3): The Greek word for "therefore" (used only here and in 1 Thess. 4:8) means literally "[as] a conclusion of emphasis."[180] Having provided such powerful examples of faith, the writer now makes a practical application to his readers (12:1). Many "witnesses"[181] continue to speak of their own personal faith and experiences, much like Abel's blood still "speaks" to us (recall 11:4). Collectively, these faithful men and women form a great "cloud" or host which looks down upon the living (so to speak) in anticipation of our own obedience of faith (see Rev. 7:9-17 for a parallel thought). Or they serve as a figurative crowd of cheering spectators who, having run their own race, now encourage those who are presently running. The faithful

---

179 This is *not* to support the centuries-old myth that these men went to some spiritual dungeon-like prison until Christ "descended into the lower parts of the earth" (Eph. 4:9). Scripture teaches no such thing. Enoch and Elijah were taken immediately into glory—whatever that glory was—and we have no reason to believe a different end awaited any other righteous man or woman prior to Christ's death. Being "made perfect" refers to that which was necessary to *allow* such men to enter glory (i.e., Christ's sacrifice), not something to be pressed into a literal, sequential timeframe. In other words, they were not "made perfect" in any manner different than we are made perfect: "by grace…through faith" (Eph. 2:8).

180 Robertson, *Word Pictures*, 432.

181 This can be translated literally "testifiers"; it is from the Greek *martures*, from which we get "martyr" (*ibid.*). In some cases, to testify of (or be a witness for) God will lead to martyrdom (Neh. 9:26, Mat. 24:9, John 16:2-3, etc.).

life is indeed a "race," not a casual stroll; "Patience [or, endurance], then, is not merely sitting down and waiting until something happens."[182]

To "lay aside every encumbrance" (12:1) is an allusion to the Greek Olympics, where the athletes ran in the nude (or nearly so), without any unnecessary clothing impeding their stride. (See similar exhortations in Luke 21:34, Col. 3:8, James 1:21, and 1 Peter 2:1.) Whatever hinders our discipleship to Christ must be removed (cf. Mat. 5:29-30); we cannot "run" with impediments, distractions, or stumbling blocks getting in the way of our progress.

"[A]nd the sin..."—not just "sin" in general, but *the* sin ("the" is in the Greek text). This undoubtedly refers to *unbelief*, the specific sin about which the writer has already warned (recall 3:12-13, 19). The entanglement or overwhelming of unbelief will ruin a Christian's effectiveness and will prevent him from reaching his intended goal (2 Tim. 2:4-5, 4:7). Instead of being encumbered with unbelief, the believer ought to "run with endurance"—with stamina, patience, perseverance, and *hope* (recall 10:36). This is not an instruction to run on our *own* power (rather than God's; see Eph. 1:19 and 2 Tim. 2:1) but to stay *focused* on running. God will do His part (bestow divine grace) but we must do our part (run with faithful endurance).

The secret to success is to "[fix] our eyes on Jesus" (12:2; recall 2:10). Thus, the *Hebrews* writer admonishes the Jewish Christians to look beyond their present distractions (and one another) and re-focus intently on Jesus. By implication, he admonishes us to do likewise (1 Tim. 4:10). "We are to look to [Christ's] holy life; to his patience and perseverance in trials; to what he endured in order to obtain the crown, and to his final success and triumph."[183] Jesus Christ is the origin (or author) and completion (or perfecter) of our faith: what we believe (and why we believe it) begins and ends with Him (Rom. 10:4).[184]

---

182 Coffman, *Commentary*, 311; bracketed words are mine.
183 Barnes, *Notes*, 291.
184 The Greek text does not have the word "our," but simply reads, "...of faith." Given the context, the meaning is the same: He is the source and completion of each

Just as we are expected to endure any present difficulties to the completion of our joy (Rom. 8:18, 2 Cor. 4:17-18, etc.), so Jesus has already done the same. Jesus did not look upon the *cross* with joy but found tremendous joy in *obeying His Father*. Whatever that obedience required, even if death on a cross (Phil. 2:7-9), He was willingly compliant: "Your will be done" (Mat. 26:39). "[D]espising [or, scorning] the shame" probably means: the Jews who crucified Jesus meant to ridicule and humiliate Him, but He was not destroyed by this, as they had hoped.[185] Instead, He turned this situation on its head and made His cross a symbol of great power, glory, and success (1 Cor. 1:18, Col. 2:15). Having been victorious over all His enemies, He "has sat down"—once again (recall 1:3), Jesus sits on His throne only because His earthly work has been completed.

"For consider Him who has endured..." (12:3)—in other words, Christ serves as a powerful example to the rest of us. His unspeakably brutal ordeal on the cross was more than compensated by His being exalted by His Father to the highest position in heaven. No one else's trials can compare to His; nonetheless, He promises that every faithful Christian will *share* in His glory, even though they will never have to pay its *cost* (Phil. 3:20-21, Rev. 3:21). These promises are given "so that [we] may not grow weary and lose heart." To lose one's heart implies feebleness, faintheartedness, and excessive doubt (Gal. 6:9); it is the opposite of faith and courage. The idea of losing heart stands in sharp contrast to the believer's confidence in Christ, our great High Priest (recall 3:6, 4:16, 10:19-23, 35).

---

individual believer's faith; He is the basis for our faith; He defines what our faith must look like and how it must develop over time. Still, "...of faith" works as well: Christ is not merely the basis for *my* faith or *your* faith but of *all* (or *every person's*) faith in Him. "The faith" (as in 1 Cor. 16:13 or Jude 1:3) refers to what is required of *any* person who calls upon Christ for salvation (Acts 4:12).

185 Consider also that being "hanged on a tree" represented a curse (Deut. 21:22-23 and Gal. 3:13-14); thus, Christ bore the reproach of one who was (said to be) cursed. "To die by crucifixion was to plumb the lowest depths of disgrace; it was a punishment reserved for those who were deemed of all men most unfit to live, a punishment for sub-men. From so degrading a death, Roman citizens were exempt by ancient statute; the dignity of the Roman name would be besmirched by being brought into association with anything so vile as the cross" (Bruce, *Commentary*, 352).

To add force to the writer's words here, we are to recall the situation about which he is writing. Certain Hebrew Christians are discouraged because of what they have had to endure for their faith in Christ; they have abandoned their heritage, possibly their families and Jewish friends, and the sacred Law of Moses. Some of them have faced suffering, reproaches, and in some cases even the seizure of their property (recall 10:32-34). Yet, they have not seen the fulfillment of all that Christ has promised them through His gospel. This is a people second-guessing their decision to leave everything behind to follow God's Son. Thus, the writer is providing strong and irrefutable encouragement to keep them focused, resilient, and unwavering in their faith. They have so much to lose by defaulting on their commitment to Christ, but they have *everything* to gain if they do not lose their faith in Him.

A Father's Discipline of His Sons (12:4-11): While the Hebrew Christians had indeed faced some great trials, and some had suffered loss for the sake of their faith, they had not yet suffered the loss of blood—i.e., their lives had been spared (12:4). Their "striving" was real, but it was not yet over—and (the writer implies) it is not time to *stop* striving.[186] Their struggle was "against sin"—whether sin in general or the specific sin of unbelief that the writer has been addressing throughout the entire epistle. Christ shed blood in His resistance of the world; many of His followers would likewise resist sin even to the point of death. The Hebrew Christians will not be prepared to follow Christ in faith— even to the point of death (Rev. 2:10)—if they allow themselves to be "encumbered" with doubt and weariness. "And hence," Milligan notes, "as their afflictions were yet comparatively light, they were the more inexcusable for their timidity and cowardice."[187]

These Christians had need of endurance, and one thing that will produce endurance is *discipline* (12:5-6). We often view "discipline" in a negative

---

[186] "Striving" is from the Greek word *antagonizomai*, "to struggle against," and alludes to Grecian contests of boxing or wrestling in which the opponents would be covered with blood from the ferocity of their struggle (Strong, *Dictionary* [electronic], G464; Barnes, *Notes*, 294). Consider Luke 13:24, Col. 1:29, and 1 Tim. 4:10 here.

[187] Milligan, *Commentary*, 346; bracketed words are mine.

sense, as an uncomfortable correction or punishment for something wrongly done. While discipline can involve this, it also refers to the structure and stability that supports and strengthens one's belief system. This involves instruction (Col. 2:6-7), diligent application of virtue (2 Peter 1:5-7), and self-mastery (2 Tim. 1:7). Unfortunately, when these habits are missing, or if one has slacked in employing them, corrective or punitive discipline will be necessary.

This is true in the present case: the Hebrew Christians were to be strong and mature, but they had instead become dull of hearing (recall 5:11-12). This is unacceptable behavior for "sons" of God—and since they *were* sons, God would *treat* them like sons and discipline them as needed. Criminals receive mere punishment, sons receive discipline; we are not to overlook the difference here. God does not give His sons what they *deserve*; He gives them (in the form of admonition, correction, or other means) what they *need*. The Scripture citation is from Prov. 3:11-12; Christ later cites from this same passage (Rev. 3:19). A father who does not discipline his son is not showing genuine *love* (12:7), since "sonship and fatherly chastisement invariably go together."[188] If God did not discipline His own sons, then it would indicate that this alleged "sonship" is in fact illegitimate: sons who are not disciplined are really not sons at all (12:8).[189] If one's sonship is questioned, then so is his inheritance (Gal. 4:7).[190]

A Christian should not assume that *any* adversity he faces is automatically godly "discipline." Sometimes it is our own guilty conscience that reads divine chastisement into a particular hardship we may be facing. Far more often, we face adversity simply because we

---

188 Lenski, *Interpretation*, 435.

189 Another possibility also exists: sons who are not disciplined have an irresponsible and unloving *father*. But in the case of God, this is impossible, since "God is love" (1 John 4:8) and is thus fully responsible toward those entrusted to Him *and* always acts in their best interest. Given this, the alternative is not even pursued here.

190 "In ancient times, the identification of legitimate children was directly connected to the inheritance of an estate, and only a man's legitimate children were considered his heirs. Under Greek law illegitimate children (i.e., children born outside of a citizen union) had no claim on their father's estate" (McClister, *Commentary*, 453).

live in a sinful world *and* because we stand opposed to that world in our faith. And, sadly, what we think is God's discipline may only be the consequences we face from our own foolish choices.

On the other hand, it appears that God is getting the Hebrew Christians' attention with very real (but undisclosed) discipline to send a strong message: *you are going in the wrong direction*. Earthly fathers discipline their sons for (ideally) good reason: to direct them away from destructive behavior and redirect them toward proper behavior. Since this is acceptable of earthly fathers, it is especially so of our heavenly Father, whose knowledge of what is "good" is far superior to that of any earthly father (12:9-10; see Mat. 7:9-11). Earthly fathers participated in bringing us into the world, but God is the "Father of spirits": He gives life to our otherworldly souls. Thus, His discipline is far more important than that of a biological parent. Earthly fathers, for all the good that they do, cannot save their children's souls; our heavenly Father has both the *ability* and *desire* to save our souls (1 Tim. 2:4). Earthly fathers prepare their children for this life, but our heavenly Father prepares us for the life to come, so that in all things "we may share His holiness." Thus, there is a direct connection between *preparedness* and *drawing near to God in holiness* (see 2 Cor. 5:5 and 1 Peter 1:13-16). No one can draw near to God who is not properly prepared for this presentation.

Of course, no one *likes* corrective discipline (12:11). It is often painful and sorrowful. Yet the outcome, when properly administered and properly received, is the refinement of our souls (Psalm 119:67, 71, and James 1:2-4). Furthermore, all such discipline is limited to this life on this earth; it is temporary and finite; it will not be necessary in the life to come. The reason for God's discipline *here* is to bring us into conformity with His own holy nature (Eph. 5:1). Once we are *with* God in the afterlife, we will have already been conformed to Him; "we will be like Him" (1 John 3:2-3)—not just in glory, but also in holy nature. Discipline produces pain, sorrow, and loss; but the ideal *result* of discipline is "the peaceful fruit of righteousness." Just as fruit takes time to mature and ripen, so the "fruit of righteousness" will not develop immediately. Yet, over time, it will be for the believer exactly what he was looking for all along.

Desired Response to God's Discipline (12:12-17): God does His part—i.e., whatever discipline is needed to redirect the soul—but the Christian must also do *his* part (12:12).[191] The writer makes another strong admonition to the recipients of his epistle: they had not finished the race, yet they were already tired and weary; they ought to be strong, but instead they were weak and appeared untrained (recall 5:11-12).

This deterioration (atrophy) of their spiritual lives threatened their inheritance with God. To "make straight paths [or, tracks] for your feet" (12:13) means to set oneself a clear and identifiable course, then stay on that course without straying or stumbling. A runner whose legs are "put out of joint" is unable to run as he ought; he will not finish the race. Hands, knees, and feet symbolize the parts of the human body that give one mobility and productivity in the physical world. The improper functioning of these robs one of his forward movements, so to speak, in life. This is as true in the spiritual context as it is in the physical: weak, under-prepared, and spiritually lame Christians will not finish their race. God's grace is the source of spiritual strength, healing, and forgiveness, but God does not do for a person what he is able (and instructed) to do for himself.

"Pursue peace with all men" (12:14)—i.e., follow after it, as though it were leading (you) in a certain direction. We are to seek heavenly peace, as with divine wisdom (see Prov. 4:4-14, for example), with active pursuit, never passive indifference. Spiritual peace is only obtainable through a right relationship with God (Rom. 5:1-2), and this relationship requires our most serious time, effort, and commitment.

But the writer here speaks to the peace we are to pursue "with all men"—i.e., the peace we have *within*, because of our right relationship with God, must be extended to others. Initially, we are to seek peace with fellow believers (Rom. 14:19); secondarily, to "all men" (see Gal. 6:9-10). Peace, rather than strife, contention, and enmity, is the noble characteristic of all genuine sons of God (Mat. 5:9). Peace (as God defines it, and for the purpose of furthering His will) is the product

---

191 The words here are like those in Prov. 4:26-27 and Isa. 35:3-4.

of heavenly wisdom; jealousy and selfish ambition are the products of human wisdom. One is the "fruit of righteousness," the other leads to division, "disorder and every evil thing"; one is of God, the other is "earthly, natural, [and] demonic" (James 3:13-18).

It is impossible to pursue peace with God without first seeking His sanctification (the process of being sanctified or made holy). Sanctification means *holiness* (see 1 Cor. 1:2, 6:11). While we have a part to play in achieving holiness (see 2 Cor. 7:1 and 1 Peter 1:13-16, for example), it is God who *makes* us holy. No one can be sanctified (made holy) apart from the work of divine grace (see Titus 3:3-7, where "justified" necessarily implies sanctification). Since no one who is unholy will "see the Lord" (i.e., stand in His presence), those who are God's people must also be holy. Sanctification implies purity, and purity is necessary to walk in fellowship with the Lord. Paul's words to Titus are appropriate here: "To the pure, all things are pure; but to those who are defiled and unbelieving, nothing is pure, but both their mind and their conscience are defiled" and thus they are rendered "worthless for any good deed" (Titus 1:15-16).

To "come short of the grace of God" (12:15) means to forfeit God's divine favor by failing to appreciate or implement it. It is, in essence, failure—a failure that, while avoidable, ruins the soul. (Remember that the writer is talking here to Christians, not the unconverted.) A Christian can "come short" of saving grace through impenitence, negligence, self-righteousness, arrogance, or simply an excessive preoccupation with lesser things. He is supposed to be strengthened by grace and grow in it (2 Tim. 2:1, 2 Peter 3:18); if he is not being strengthened, he is weakening; if he is not growing, he is dying. Disqualification is a real possibility, even for those who have preached God's word to others (1 Cor. 9:27, in principle).

A "root of bitterness" (12:15) refers to the foothold that sin makes in a person's heart: it begins as a root, searching for a firm attachment, but grows into an insidious and noxious weed when it "springs up."[192]

---

192 James Macknight writes: "A root of bitterness is a person, utterly corrupted, and

The allusion here is to Deut. 29:14-21, where Israel was sternly warned against any apostasy (i.e., falling away from the truth [of God]), which is the same danger being warned against here. "Trouble" in this context calls to mind Achan and the trouble he caused Israel—and the wretched end he faced because of his unbelief (Josh. 7:22-26). The point is: God's grace, when one fully embraces it, makes him invincible to falling away from the truth (or "stumbling," as in 2 Peter 1:10-11). However, God cannot help the Christian whose heart is filled (or defiled) with sin. It is not as though God's power is in any way diminished but that He cannot have fellowship with evil (see Isa. 59:1-2).

Scripture does not have any approving things to say about Esau (12:16-17). Esau represents the secular, earth-bound, worldly mentality that stands in opposition to God, just as the Edomites (descendants of Esau) several times stood opposed to Israel (Exod. 17:8-16, Num. 20:14-21, etc.). The writer does not mean that Esau himself was sexually immoral (although this might be a reference to his marriage choices; see Gen. 26:34-35). Yet fornicators, idolaters, and unholy people fall into the same category: they all have a disregard for what is proper and sacred.[193] Esau demonstrated this disregard when he sold his divine birthright for a single meal. What he forfeited, he never recovered, even though later he bitterly regretted it (see Gen. 27:30-40).[194] In a similar vein, the Hebrew

---

who by his errors and vices corrupts others" (quoted in Coffman, *Commentary*, 324). Just as the root ultimately reveals its true nature in the form of a plant, the corrupted soul will be revealed in that person's earthly actions (Mat. 7:15-20, in principle).

193 One must wonder why the writer brings up *sexual sins* (implied in "immoral") to a group of Hebrew Christians who very unlikely had anything to do with these. But immorality is the natural result of a "godless person," as the apostle Paul revealed (Rom. 1:21-27). Perhaps the writer is saying: "If you forfeit your reward in Christ by turning away from Him—something only a godless person would do—then do not be surprised at what kind of illicit behaviors this will ultimately produce, even in yourselves." In any case, the warning has full force to us today: any godless attitude, behavior, or belief system is inherently *immoral* in nature. Esau serves as a timeless parable of what this looks like and what one loses in the process.

194 The "no place to repent" phrase brings us back to the thoughts discussed in 10:26-27. Esau lost all opportunity to regain his first-born inheritance since Isaac would not change his mind (see Barnes, *Notes*, 304; Coffman, *Commentary*, 327-328). This is not a comment on the state of Esau's eternal soul; nonetheless, it appears that a person can reach a point in his lifetime when he forfeits all opportunity for repentance to God and

Christians were attempting to forfeit their inheritance with God for an inferior and obsolete religion (Judaism)—a bowl of stew in comparison to the promises of inheritance with Christ.

The Unshakable Kingdom (12:18-29)

The Physical Mt Sinai (12:18-21): Having made strong statements, the writer now (characteristically) begins relaxing his approach and moves toward positive things. The purpose of his instruction is to help prepare his readers for their presentation before God (12:18-21). He likens this to the occasion of Israel's presentation before God at Mt Sinai (Exod. 19 – 24). On that occasion, God needed to contrast His holy nature against that of worldly Israel—and He did so with a frightening display of fire, smoke, thunder, and lightning. Three major points here:

- Israel had to *prepare* themselves to be in God's presence (Exod. 19:10-11, 15). They could not simply "show up" in their casual clothes, so to speak (like so many people do today for church services), but they had to be washed, separated from sexual activity with their spouses, and "be ready" to meet the Lord. God was not coming to meet *them*, but *they* were coming to Sinai to meet *Him*.
- The Israelites could not come any closer to God than He allowed. Boundaries were set up at the base of Mt Sinai to prevent any person (or even an animal) from touching the mountain, which was designated a holy place because of God's presence there (Exod. 19:12-13). This separation magnified the sacred distance between unholy people (i.e., *all of us*) and a holy God.
- God spoke His ten commandments to the people audibly, with His own voice (Exod. 20:1, 22). This thundering sound—accompanied with the smoke, lightning, and actual thunder—proved to be too much for the people. They begged Moses to speak with God himself rather than them having to endure this any further (Exod. 20:18-

---

will lose his soul. Just because we cannot know *when* (or *if*) someone crosses this line does not mean the line does not exist or cannot be crossed.

22; see Deut. 5:4-5). Yet so intimidating was God's presence on the mountain that even Moses was terrified (12:21).[195]

God's holy presence demanded the Israelites' utmost reverence and respect; He threatened them with *death* if they failed to obey Him. Thus, a careless or unbelieving person—i.e., one with a disposition like Esau's—would have been destroyed. God wanted to impress upon Israel that He was *unapproachable* apart from two things: His gracious *invitation* (like what He provided through Moses—see Exod. 3:12) and Israel's own *holy conduct* (which required visible demonstration).

The God whom we approach now—in prayer, spiritual communion, and our collective worship—has not changed. As He required Israel to be *prepared* to approach Him, so He requires us to be prepared to approach Him; as He kept a sacred distance between Himself and Israel, so we are to remember that He is in heaven and we are on earth (Eccles. 5:2, Mat. 6:9); and as He spoke to Israel with His own voice, so He speaks to us "in His Son" (recall 1:1-2). Even though we cannot "touch" the spiritual Mt Zion (as an Israelite could literally touch Mt Sinai), nonetheless we are still dealing with a God who demands our highest reverence and respect. Even though God speaks to us "in His Son," it is still *God speaking*. While Jesus' demeanor seems far less threatening than what the Israelites encountered at Sinai, we are not to think that His authority or power has diminished.

Again, we do not serve a different God now than Israel did, which means we ought not to be any less reverent than they were to be. We may have a different *perspective* of God since we have seen His "grace upon grace" in the Lord Jesus Christ (John 1:16-18), but we ought never to forget the absolute *holiness* of God. We can approach the Father through the Son (John 14:6) but otherwise God remains unapproachable, especially in our present physical state (1 Tim. 6:15-16). As with Israel, no person

---

195 There is no record of Moses' reaction to God's presence at Sinai on the occasion being mentioned. Later, in Deut. 9:19, Moses admits that he was terrified of God's displeasure, but this was after the golden calf incident. One of two things are possible here: the writer assumes that Moses trembled along with the rest of the people (see Exod. 19:16); or the writer is drawing from some extra-biblical source of information.

today can approach God whom He has not invited to do so. Our invitation is through His gospel, by which He calls all people to Himself (Acts 2:39, Rom. 8:29-30, 2 Thess. 2:14, etc.).

The Spiritual Mt Zion (12:22-24): "But you have come to Mount Zion..."—i.e., not a physical mountain but a spiritual one, the foundation for the holy *city of believers*. "Zion" is the ancient name of one of the hills of Jerusalem and is sometimes used to refer to the entire city (Psalm 2:6, 132:13, etc.). In prophetic context, however, it symbolized the future gathering place of God's glorified people on earth (Isa. 2:2-4, 51:1-5, 59:19-21, Joel 2:1-32, Rev. 14:1-3, etc.). No longer is the literal city of Jerusalem relevant (see John 4:21-24); Christ has built a new "temple-city"—His church—in which all the redeemed who live on earth will dwell (Rev. 14:1-3).

To be clear: "Zion" represents Christ's divine authority; it is the "rock" upon which He will build His church (Mat. 16:18). "Jerusalem" represents the church itself which He has founded upon this "rock"/mountain. It is a symbolic portrayal of the *physical* church—the assembly of the global brotherhood of Christ on earth—and not (yet) the *heavenly* church which will enter eternal glory after the world has run its course (as in Rev. 21:1ff).

In contrast to the severe, primitive, and earthly context of physical Mt Sinai, Christians have come to a "mountain" of glory, majesty, and thrilling anticipation (12:22-24):

- It is the **"city of the living God"**: This does not merely designate a meeting place but an organized, established, and spiritual community in which to dwell, to live securely forever (recall 11:10). The depiction here is not of the final dwelling place of the redeemed but their holy gathering on the earth—one people, one city, and one King and High Priest, all on one "mountain."
- It is **"the heavenly Jerusalem"**: This is not the literal city of Jerusalem, but one based on its (OT) significance and symbolism. Just as God chose Jerusalem as the place where His people would

worship Him (compare Deut. 12:1-7 and 1 Kings 11:13), so the "heavenly" Jerusalem, which is Christ's physical church on earth, is where God's people will worship Him. The physical Jerusalem is bound to this world and enslaved to the Law of Moses; "But the Jerusalem above [i.e., the transcendent city—MY WORDS] is free; she is our mother. ... And you brethren, like Isaac, are children of promise" (Gal. 4:26, 28).

❏ Christians have come to:
- **"myriads of angels"**: God's Presence is always surrounded by a great abundance and diversity of *life*, including many ministers, attendants, and "living creatures" (Rev. 5:11). These angelic beings also minister to the redeemed of Zion (recall 1:14). It is difficult to know whether this great company of angels is with the church on earth or with God in heaven. While both scenarios are defended by commentators, the construction of the Greek text favors the latter.[196] While the Law was officiated by angels in a terrifying way, this present scene depicts a festive scene with joy and celebration.[197]
- **"the general assembly"**: The Greek word translated "assembly" here is not *ekklesia*, as we would normally expect, but *paneguris*, which refers not to a modest assembly but a very large one, as though an entire population of people have been brought together.[198] Spiritual Zion is not a small "city" but an immense one which defies physical dimensions (Rev. 7:9 and 21:10-17).
- the **"church of the firstborn who ... heaven"**: The Firstborn is Christ (Rom. 8:29, Col. 1:18, and Rev. 1:5), indicating His pre-eminence before the redeemed. His "firstborn" status is determined by virtue of His being the only begotten Son of God and His resurrection—the first of its kind (never to die again). But the "firstborn" in a general sense may refer to the redeemed (here, *ekklesia*), as the "first fruits" idea also is used of both Christ and His people (compare 1 Cor. 15:20 and James 1:18, for example). This group of people stands before all humankind as

---

196 Barnes, *Notes*, 308.
197 Vincent, *Word Studies* (electronic), on 12:22.
198 Strong, *Dictionary* (electronic), G3831.

those who are (spiritually) "a people of [God's] own possession" (Titus 2:14) and fellow heirs of God. The fact that these people are "enrolled" means that have a *right* to be in this church (Luke 10:20, Phil. 4:3, and Rev. 3:5), an idea consistent with being "sealed" of God (Eph. 4:30, Rev. 7:1-3).[199] While Christians' names are enrolled in heaven, the scene here (in 12:23) is not *yet* of heaven but depicts the great company of believers who yet remain on the earth.

- **"God, the Judge of all"**: While a "judge" usually has a negative connotation (i.e., as one who hands out sentences of punishment), in this case the meaning is positive. God, as Judge of all men, *does* condemn those who do not believe or do not obey, yet He will exonerate His own people (Rom. 2:9-11, 2 Thess. 1:6-10, etc.). God is also the Judge of His church—not to condemn His saints but to declare them legally justified and therefore innocent. If "God is the one who justifies" us, then "who is the one who condemns?" (Rom. 8:33-34).

- **"the spirits of {the} righteous made perfect"**: No one can *be* righteous without having been *made* perfect, which requires nothing short of an act of God. Just as God credited (or reckoned) Abraham as righteous because of his faith (Rom. 4:1-5), so all believers are made righteous by God, having been "made perfect" through the atoning blood of Christ, who Himself was "made perfect" through His flawless obedience (recall 5:8-10).

- **"Jesus, ... new covenant"**: This covenant of salvation is superior to all those previously made, and God's covenant with Israel in particular. All prior covenants having to do with salvation are *summed up* in this one, just as all things are summed up in Christ (Eph. 1:9-10). Those who dwell on Mt Zion (the church on earth) are those who are identified with God through the covenant which was brought to life by the uncorrupted blood of Christ.

---

199 There also seems to be an underlying contrast to faithless Esau, who was also a firstborn son but thought little of such privileged distinction.

- **"the sprinkled blood, which … Abel"**: Abel's blood, though it speaks well of Abel himself (recall 11:4), cannot "speak" for the rest of us. Even he had to offer up animal (blood) sacrifices for his own sins, and though he died as a martyr, his blood saved no one. Christ, however, had no sins and thus served as a worthy offering for *us*: a perfect, unblemished, and once-for-all sacrifice. His blood "speaks" for us in the sense that it covers our sins, which is the meaning of atonement. His blood is in every sense superior to that of Abel's.

The writer here describes a scene which seems both present and future all at once. Those who are "in Christ" join with this great throng of the redeemed by faith and in promise. It is *real*, but it remains (for Christians in this life) conditioned upon our completion of the "race that is set before us" (recall 12:1). Once our work on earth is done and we enter our "Sabbath rest," however, this promise will be a visible reality (recall 4:9). The writer thus implores his readers to consider very seriously what he is saying: *Zion—not Sinai—is the "mountain" to which you were called in Christ!* It is vastly superior to what was defined in the first covenant in every respect.[200] Those who wanted to return to an inferior system would *forfeit* their participation in this great spiritual assembly.

The Need for Reverence and Awe (12:25-29): The writer reiterates a point made earlier: Moses warned the Israelites not to disobey God, lest they face the punishment of death (12:25; recall 2:1-3).[201] But Moses warned from the earth, threatening physical execution; how much more threatening, then, are God's warnings from heaven, threatening the execution (so to speak) of one's soul! Remember, too, He through whom God has now spoken—His Son (recall 1:2)—and we are to "listen to Him!" (Mat. 17:5). To "refuse" God means to stubbornly disbelieve His power and His promises, even though He has provided sufficient

---

200 A student of the Bible would do well to consider Paul's allegory in Gal. 4:17-31 regarding this.

201 The implication here is also that of the generation of Israelites who died in the wilderness, who failed to listen to the voice of God as revealed through His servant Moses (Num. 14:22-23; see 1 Cor. 10:5).

reason to believe in them (recall 3:12-19). It is impossible to refuse God's salvation through His Son and be pleasing to Him all at once. Such people may *think* they are serving God but in fact do not have any fellowship with Him (John 16:2-3, in principle).

While God's voice shook Mt Sinai, He will once again shake all creation (12:26-27), indicating the *removal* of such things (i.e., the end of the physical system). To "shake" here (quoting from Hag. 2:6-7) implies not only God's sovereignty over whatever is shaken but also the temporariness or destructibility of such things.[202] The Creator is eternal and indestructible—He cannot be "shaken" by anyone or anything— but He has the authority and ability to "shake" (or remove) all that has been created. "The final shaking that began with the coming of Jesus is going on now and will be finished when he returns. The entire universe will shake in this final great catastrophe. This is a sifting process that will leave only those things that are eternal."[203]

This passage seems to serve as a dual prophecy: it speaks of an ultimate "shaking [or, sifting]," but this does not prevent other lesser (but significant) upheavals in the meantime. One such upheaval was clearly the destruction of Jerusalem (AD 70), which marked the termination of the Law of Moses, its sacrificial system, the Levitical priesthood, and the privileged status of Israel toward all other nations. All these things God once created; all these things God has since removed. But the kingdom of God—the reign and realm of Christ's authority in which the church has been established—*will not* be shaken, since it is eternal and indestructible (Dan. 7:13-14). As the Jewish system ended in a catastrophic event, so the physical universe will end in a cataclysmic destruction (2 Peter 3:7-12): the created world will be destroyed and

---

202 Haggai's prophecy does not refer to the same event as what the *Hebrews* writer refers, although they both use the same language. Haggai's prophecy referred to the end of the four-nation Gentile empire (see Dan. 2:31-35), in which the throne of David and the city of Jerusalem would be, in their *spiritual* contexts, fulfilled in Christ and His church. Here (in 12:26) the perspective looks to the end of time when God will finally and cataclysmically "shake" the entire physical system, to bring it to an end, so that the only thing that remains thereafter is His kingdom (12:27-28).

203 JFB, *Commentary* (electronic), on 12:26-27.

only the kingdom of God will remain, unscathed. The essential point is this: the Hebrew Christians are considering a return to that which was about to be *destroyed* while abandoning that which *cannot be destroyed*.

"Therefore...let us show gratitude" (12:28)—not fear, doubt, unbelief, or indifference. Ingratitude and irreverence always go together: one leads to the other. In other words, instead of critiquing God's heavenly plans through finite, earthly perspectives, Christians are to *give thanks* that He has invited us into His eternal and majestic dwelling place (John 14:1-3). "Acceptable service [or, worship]" is reminiscent of Rom. 12:1-2; both passages refer to the priestly action of offering sacrifices to God. While Christ is our sin offering and burnt offering, still we are to offer personal sacrifices of faith, humility, devotion, and good works. Christians, "as living stones, are being built up as a spiritual house for a holy priesthood, to offer up spiritual sacrifices acceptable to God through Jesus Christ" (1 Peter 2:5).

Such holy and priestly service must be with "reverence" and "awe"—i.e., with *devout respect* and with a *healthy fear of God* (Prov. 1:7, Eccles. 12:13, etc.). While some Hebrew Christians thought they could serve God adequately through the Law of Moses, forsaking the holy assembly on Mt Zion displayed *unbelief, irreverence,* and *ingratitude*, not "acceptable service." The same God who consumed unbelievers with fire long ago (Lev. 10:1-3 and Num. 16:31-35) will also—in due time—destroy those who are ungrateful and irreverent to Him in His church (12:29).

This perspective seems lost on so many Christians today, who—in their attitude, conduct, dress, and casual approach to church assemblies—embrace a "come as you are" mentality toward collective worship. The lessons in both Exod. 19 and Heb. 12, not to mention elsewhere in Scripture, paint a very different approach—one to which we all would do well to pay attention. Solemnity, sacredness, reverence, and preparedness are the biblical hallmarks of the assemblies of God's people.

Section Five:
Final Admonitions
(13:1–25)

Christian Responsibilities
(13:1–19)

Nearing the end of his epistle, the writer of *Hebrews* makes some final admonitions to his readers. His focus is twofold: moral *purity* (to Christ) and moral *responsibility* (to Christians). "Let love of the brethren continue" (13:1)—lit., "keep on loving each other as brothers [in Christ]."[204] This describes a continuous action, not a random or incidental one. There is a necessary link between one's devotion to Christ and his love for God's people. "Anyone of the readers who would be inclined to give up Christ and to revert to Judaism would promptly show that decline in faith by coldness and indifference to his Christian brethren."[205] Brotherly love is one of the defining traits of Christians; it is impossible to represent Christ rightly without demonstrating this. This same admonition is found elsewhere in the NT:

- "A new commandment I give to you, that you love one another, even as I have loved you, that you also love one another. By this all men will know that you are My disciples, if you have love for one another." (John 13:34-35)
- "Let love be without hypocrisy. ... Be devoted to one another in brotherly love; give preference to one another in honor...." (Rom. 12:9-10)
- "Now as to the love of the brethren, you have no need for anyone to write to you, for you yourselves are taught by God to love one

---

204 The phrase "love of the brethren" comes from a single Greek word *philadelphia*, which is used four other times in the NT (Rom. 12:10, 1 Thess. 4:9, 1 Peter 1:22, and 2 Peter 1:7) (Strong, *Dictionary* [electronic], G5360).
205 Lenski, *Interpretation*, 468.

another; for indeed you do practice it toward all the brethren who are in all Macedonia." (1 Thess. 4:9)
- "Since you have in obedience to the truth purified your souls for a sincere love of the brethren, fervently love one another from the heart...." (1 Peter 1:22)
- "If someone says, 'I love God,' and hates his brother, he is a liar; for the one who does not love his brother whom he has seen, cannot love God whom he has not seen. And this commandment we have from Him, that the one who loves God should love his brother also." (1 John 4:20-21)

We are to "do good" to *all* people, but "especially to those who are of the household of the faith" (Gal. 6:10) and "without complaint" (1 Peter 4:9). One who will not properly care for his own spiritual family is not prepared to deal rightly with those outside of it (1 Tim. 5:8, in principle). A specific manifestation of Christian love and kindness is *hospitality* (13:2). The Greek word for "hospitality" [*philoxenia*] literally means "kind to guests" or "lover of strangers." "Strangers" in this context specifically refers to *brethren* who are (previously) unknown to us, such as travelers or missionaries (as in 3 John 1:5-8). The traveling Christians of the first century faced difficulties that we may have trouble appreciating. Inns were expensive, of ill-repute, or simply scarce in number; thieves laid in wait on the highways; travelers faced wild animals and inclement weather; people lost their lives just "traveling." Thus, the expressed need for hospitality is greater (here) than we might first realize.

The reference to "angels" (13:2) undoubtedly alludes to Abraham and Lot's kindness toward angelic messengers in Gen. 18—19. Many Christians have taught from this passage, however, that "strangers" *we* meet are sometimes angels in disguise, roaming the earth and intersecting with our lives. Such fanciful interpretation goes well beyond the intent and context of this passage. There is nothing else in the NT to support this.[206] On the other hand, it *may* be true that God does allow

---

206 "The reference to angels does not mean that Christians should practice hospitality with the express hope of entraining angels. It is instead another way of

anonymous saints (and even those who are not saints) to cross our paths to give us opportunity to show kindness and hospitality. And it is *always* true that whatever we do for Christ's brethren, we do for Him also (Mat. 25:40).

"Prisoners," likewise, are not common criminals, as people tend to interpret this (13:3). This passage is allegedly the basis for modern prison ministries carried out by Christians and churches. While sharing the gospel with guilty criminals is noble, this passage refers to people jailed for their *faith*, not their crimes.[207] One who takes care of such prisoners ought to do so with sympathy and compassion, as though he himself were imprisoned (as might be the case someday). "[I]n the body" seems to refer to the physical flesh, not the body of Christ; in other words, "Remember those who are suffering physical afflictions for the sake of Christ and identify with them, since you also are in the flesh and thus susceptible to these same afflictions." When one member suffers, all members are to suffer with him (Rom. 12:15, 1 Cor. 12:26). In remembering "strangers" and "prisoners," the writer is saying, "Show godly love to fellow Christian travelers, whether or not you had previously met them; reach out to Christians who need your care and are unable to provide for their own needs."

Christians are to practice especially in the privacy of their homes and the intimacy of their marriages (13:4). Marriage is a divinely created institution and a holy union (Mat. 19:6). In effect, it is also both a legal and accommodating provision for the sexual needs of a man and a woman (1 Cor. 7:1-2). "Bed" here (13:4) is a euphemism for the sexual activity between a husband and his wife. "Fornicators" and "adulterers" are mentioned separately here since they are not identical (see 1 Cor. 6:9). All adulterers are fornicators, but not all fornicators are adulterers. Fornication is any sexually immoral or deviant behavior, regardless (or

---

saying that those who show hospitality to all often gain unexpected benefits from their guests" (Lightfoot, *Jesus Christ Today*, 247).

207 This fact recalls what was said in 10:34; see Mat. 25:39, Acts 28:30, and 2 Tim. 1:16-17. "Moreover, imprisonment was not a form of punishment in the Roman legal system. Prisons were for people who were awaiting trial, or who were awaiting execution" (McClister, *Commentary*, 493).

even in the absence) of a pre-existing relationship. Adultery specifically involves one who is already in a covenant (marriage) relationship; it is the corruption *of* that covenant through some form of treachery (Mal. 2:14-16) that involves a third party—someone outside of his or her marriage. (The writer here refers only to sexual adultery, but not every form of adultery is sexual; see Mat. 5:27-28.) "God will judge" those who practice such things since this contradicts the purity of the church (1 Thess. 4:3-8).

Christian love is an excellent virtue and required of God's people. "Love of money" (13:5a) is an unholy love that, if practiced, leads to the ruin of God's people. This "love" seeks contentment in something other than God. Money represents human authority or man-made institutions; the love of money implies a greater trust or confidence in human power than in God's (see Luke 12:15, 16:14-15). Not only this, but no one can love both money and God equally; one loyalty will always be greater than the other (Mat. 6:24). One who chooses to love money (i.e., wealth or earthly securities of any kind) automatically compromises his love for God and inevitably engages in other evils as well (1 Tim. 6:10).

In contrast, Christians are to learn to be content with their circumstances. This does not mean that we can never seek to improve our situation (see 1 Cor. 7:21, in principle) or obtain a higher paying job. Earning money or having money is not the same thing as an unholy *love* for money: one is a responsibility or stewardship; the other is a corruption of the heart. Contentment, in this context, means finding satisfaction in *God* rather than in anything (or anyone) in this world (1 Tim. 6:6, Phil. 4:11-12, etc.). Human pride seeks satisfaction in something other than God; all sin is the result of dissatisfaction with God's provisions. As divine grace is sufficient for the soul (2 Cor. 12:9), so divine providence is sufficient for our well-being. "The love of money is just as much an evil desire as the sexual lust that can violate marriage."[208]

---

[208] JFB, *Commentary* (electronic), on 13:5.

Seeking sexual satisfaction outside of marriage (i.e., defiling the marriage bed) corrupts both the violator's soul and the holy union he has with his wife. Seeking satisfaction in money—because of an unholy love for it—will ultimately disappoint and leads to the spiritual ruin of those who do this. In strong contrast, the Lord will *never* disappoint us or *fail* to save us (13:5b-6). (The writer quotes from Deut. 31:6, 8, or Josh 1:5, then from Psalm 118:6.)

Such encouragements apply generally and timelessly to God's people everywhere. The connection to the previous admonitions may be this: spouses can fail, and money *will* fail, but God will never fail. He is our Rock, our Shield, and our Security. This is especially comforting when dealing with ungodly people who trouble us (Christians) for practicing our faith. Peter's words are parallel to this: "Who is there to harm you if you prove zealous for what is good? But even if you should suffer for the sake of righteousness, you are blessed. And do not fear their intimidation, and do not be troubled..." (1 Peter 3:13-14). Even though Christians may be physically threatened by and are often at the mercy of godless men, these cannot destroy our faith or touch our souls. While *internal lusts* and *illicit desires* can corrupt our heart (James 1:13-16), no *external threat* can corrupt our salvation (Luke 12:4-7, Rom. 8:35-39).

Those Who Refuse Christ's Supremacy (13:7-14): Instead of returning to Jerusalem and its religion, the Hebrew Christians are to abandon that life altogether. The reason for this would soon be abundantly and historically clear (when divine judgment descended upon the nation of Israel in AD 70). Thus, the writer admonishes them to "remember those who led you" to Christ (13:7), rather than those who lead away from Him, or the sentimental attachment that they may have toward Judaism. These Christian leaders likely includes church elders, since they are mentioned twice more in this same chapter (13:17, 24); yet in this context it may also include teachers and missionaries of the gospel. In essence, it includes whoever "[speaks] the word of God" to others as a means of converting them to disciples of Christ (see Col. 1:3-8 regarding Epaphras, for example).

To "remember" these faithful men may mean that they have died and thus gained what was promised (recall 10:36). In any case, the point is that those who led the Hebrews to Christ have acted honorably and faithfully to God—and thus the Hebrews have a moral responsibility to follow their example (1 Cor. 11:1, Phi. 4:9, etc.). The opposite is also true: whoever would lead them *away* from Christ—even though he claims to be "of God"—must be rejected as an impostor. The writer has already warned his readers of following in the footsteps of disobedient Israelites (recall 4:11); there is no greater disobedience than to reject (or recant one's faith in) God's Son. Thus, there is no excuse for following either those who teach error or practice disobedience. Instead, all believers are admonished to imitate those who live by faith in Christ as well as those who have died in faith to Him.

While earthly leaders—like all men—appear for a little while and then fade away, there is one Leader who does not: Jesus Christ (13:8). He is "the same" throughout all time; He is the true and universal *constant* in whom there is no variation, failure, or disappointment. He is the infallible and indisputable "Yes" (or "Amen") of God (2 Cor. 1:19-20, Rev. 3:14). Since He does not change, neither does His gospel. As the head of His church, Christ presides over all believers; as King over the entire universe, He presides over everything that has been created (Col. 1:15-18). People may disappoint us—even if that disappointment (to us) is in their deaths—but Christ will not. Even the Law of Moses was disappointing, in that it could not remove sins "once for all." But Christ's sacrifice has left nothing undone and satisfies God's requirement for our atonement completely.

The final, most explicit warning is connected to the above fact: *since Christ does not change or disappoint, there is absolutely no reason to turn away from Him* (13:9). Those who are "carried away" by lesser things have not fixed their eyes on the Author and Perfecter of faith (recall 12:2), the Apostle and High Priest of our confession (recall 3:1). "[V]aried and strange teachings [or, doctrines]" may refer to the many formalities and traditions of Judaism which were added to the Law as though equal to it (see Mat. 15:3-9). This may have specific reference to dietary restrictions (because of 13:10), but it may also refer to any teachings that are foreign (or "strange") to the gospel of Christ. While the writer likely has Judaizing teachers in mind, this passage has broad application and can refer to all teachings that conflict with apostolic instruction.

Regardless, food and rituals have never *by themselves* been a measurement of fellowship with God (Rom. 14:17). Such external things do not create righteousness or substitute for moral purity (Col. 2:20-23). "In fact, the whole principle of attaching religious value to material food was inconsonant with the essence of Christianity."[209] "[T]hose who were so occupied" refers to the ancient priests who officiated over thousands of sacrifices on the altar. Those sacrifices, necessary as they were at the time, were never the source of spiritual renewal or inward change. God's grace, however, *does* transform the believer's heart to bring about a genuine inward transformation (2 Cor. 4:16, Rom. 12:1-2, 2 Tim. 2:1, etc.).

"We have an altar from which those…have no right to eat" (13:10). The Levitical priesthood has been superseded (and thus made obsolete) by Christ's high priesthood (recall 8:13). Thus, to continue to partake of that obsolete system, altar, and offerings is offensive to Christ and to the Father whose divine oath has established His new priesthood (recall 7:28). The Christian's "altar" is *Christ on His cross*—a stumbling block to unbelieving Jews and foolishness to the worldly wise (1 Cor. 1:23). Our sacrifice is a *Person*, not an animal; we partake of *His* flesh and drink *His* blood in our remembrance of Him (John 6:53-58, Luke 22:19-20).[210]

---

209 Bruce, *Commentary*, 398.

210 While Jesus (in John 6) did *not* speak of or describe the Lord's Supper directly, one cannot help but make a connection between the two ideas. Jesus spoke to the Jews of internalizing His character and His doctrine; yet later He instructed His disciples to "remember" Him in a simple memorial that symbolizes the eating of His body and drinking of His blood. An unbeliever—a non-follower of Christ—has no right to participate in this memorial. It should be noted, too, that the *Hebrews* writer makes no mention of the Lord's Supper, either here or elsewhere, so we should not assume he is saying, "Unbelievers have no right to partake of the Lord's Supper." While this statement is true, it is not his point and therefore should not be our point, either.

Hebrew Christians have *no purpose* to partake of the Levitical offerings; yet those who refuse Christ—in the present context, those who cling to the old system—have *no right* to partake of this superior offering.[211] These two systems are incompatible; only one of them is approved by God.

The sacrifice to which the writer specifically refers is a *sin offering* (13:11-12; see Lev. 4:11-12). Those for whom the sin offering was made could not eat the meat of the animal so sacrificed; they could not benefit or profit from their own sin. The offering that bore the sins for *all* people, as in the Day of Atonement sin offering for the nation of Israel, had to be taken "outside the camp"—that is, separated from the holy assembly (Exod. 19:14, Lev. 4:13-21, 16:11-14, and 27).[212] Sin is a contaminant and defilement; whatever animal was used in the atonement process was polluted by the sin that it "covered," so that it (the animal's body) had to be fully destroyed by burning. This proves that the animal's body (and, by implication, its blood) was insufficient to *remove* sin (10:4) since its body became corrupted (cursed) like the sins it bore.

Christ's sacrifice follows the same pattern as the sin offerings but succeeds where those offerings never could. His body was offered as the *once for all* sin offering and taken "outside the gate" (of Jerusalem) to die (Luke 13:33, John 19:20). Yet because He was a divine Person, He was able to offer a *perfect* sacrifice, being able to absorb the *penalty* for sin completely in Himself. While He "became [or, represented] a curse for us" (Gal. 3:13), He Himself was not accursed.[213] His body did

---

211 The gospel makes a clear distinction between the people of the "true circumcision" (i.e., Christians) and the people of physical circumcision (i.e., unbelieving Jews) who are under a curse; see Rom. 2:28-29, Gal. 6:12-16, Phil. 3:2-3, and Rev. 2:9.

212 "In this context the 'camp' stands for the established fellowship and ordinances of Judaism. To abandon them, with all their shared associations inherited from remote antiquity, was a hard thing, but it was a necessary thing. They had been accustomed to think of the 'camp' and all that was inside it as sacred, while everything outside it was profane and unclean. … [Yet] what was formerly sacred was now unhallowed, because Jesus had been expelled from it; what was formerly unhallowed was now sacred, because Jesus was there" (Bruce, *Commentary*, 403).

213 We see the same effect in Jesus' healing of, say, a leper (Mat. 8:2-3). According

not become corrupted in the process of atoning for our sins. This is why His flesh did not decay (Acts 2:29-33) and is also why we symbolically eat His body and drink His blood through the partaking of the Lord's Supper (1 Cor. 11:23-26). We could not eat the "flesh" or drink the "blood" of a dead, rotting corpse; in partaking of a *living Savior*, we eat and drink of Him who imparts *life* to us.

No animal that was offered on the ancient altar ever resurrected from its death, but Jesus died on the cross and was buried, then was resurrected to live again and never die. His newness of life is proof positive that His body and blood were sufficient for absolute atonement for the sins of men.

"So, let us go out to Him" (13:13)—i.e., the Hebrew Christians, rather than return to the Law of Moses, must separate themselves from those who practice it in defiance of Christ. By supporting the priestly sacrifices offered within Jerusalem, these Christians identified with those who were under a curse (Luke 19:41-44, 21:20-24). (The curse was upon Jerusalem specifically, but included the entire Jewish nation—i.e., all those unbelieving Jews who rejected Jesus as their Messiah.) Just as men treated Jesus as an outcast and took Him "outside the gate," so the Christian must bear his own mistreatment by unbelievers and take his place alongside Him.

As with the Hebrew Christians, so it is with us: whatever shame or hardship is necessary in identifying with Christ, we must accept this as part of our discipleship to Him. This is what it means to "take up [our] cross" for Him (Mat. 16:24). Christ's "reproach" refers to His having been crucified as a blasphemer and a criminal; the Christian also endures a type of crucifixion in his discipleship (Gal. 2:20, Phil. 3:8-11, etc.). We, like the faithful who have gone before us, must not be seeking

---

to the Law, since a leper is unclean (Lev. 13:45-46), whoever touches a leper also becomes unclean and must be ritually purified. Yet Jesus did not become unclean because He possessed the power to *heal* rather than merely *touch*. In a real sense, He overcame the leper's uncleanness by removing it entirely (see also Luke 7:11-15). Similarly, Jesus overcomes the sinner's uncleanness by removing his sin entirely, having absorbed *in Himself* the justice required for it.

an earthly city for a permanent home but one "which is to come," one which is not even of this world (recall 11:13-16).

What Is Expected of Believers (13:15-19): While Christ has offered up a sacrifice for our sins, Christians are to offer up a "sacrifice of praise to God" (13:15). Our sacrifices are never to compare with Christ's once-for-all sacrifice. Even so, these are necessary to render an "acceptable service" of worship (recall 12:28). The "fruit of lips" can mean any spoken praise or thanksgiving as well as prayers (Phil. 4:4-6), songs (Eph. 5:19, Col. 3:16-17), confessions of faith (Mat. 10:32), and all "spiritual sacrifices [which are] acceptable to God through Jesus Christ" (1 Peter 2:5, bracketed words added). Spoken praise is necessary, but the ultimate praise to Christ is demonstrated through "doing good and sharing," and especially with those who belong to Him (13:16; see Mat. 25:37-40, Gal. 6:9-10). Likewise, the greatest form of gratitude to God is in the form of our obedience.

"Obey…and submit" (13:17)—i.e., accept the counsel of your spiritual leaders and voluntarily put yourselves under their oversight. Given the context, "leaders" here refers to church elders; no other men "watch over your souls" or "give an account" in this manner. The word "rule" means "those who have rule over you"; here it indicates *managerial oversight* (as in Acts 20:28, 1 Thess. 5:12, 1 Tim. 3:4-5, and 5:17) and not superiority in rank, worth, or human nature. To "watch" over someone's soul cannot mean to lord oneself over that person, or to impose upon him in any inappropriate or unchristian way (1 Peter 5:2-3).

Often, this passage (13:17) is interpreted to read: "Obey the authority of the elders." Being authorized to do something (i.e., to abide by and enforce laws already made) and having authority to legislate something (i.e., to unilaterally make new laws) are two different things. While elders are authorized to *oversee* a group, this does not translate to having *authority* over the group—to act with independent and binding authority. Nowhere in the NT does it say that elders are to exercise their *own* authority. They are to shepherd their "flock," but they do not own the flock; they are to serve as managers, not reign as dictators; they are to nurture souls, not flash badges and brandish weapons (so to speak) as sheriffs. Congregations are to "submit" to their elders by *allowing themselves* to be governed by these men whom they have appointed for this very purpose.[214] Likewise, elders are to submit themselves in humility to the needs of the congregation (Eph. 5:21, Phil. 2:1-5). Elders are not kings or despots; they are not above fair criticism or questioning.[215]

Elders *do* have a responsibility to "watch over" the souls of their congregation (13:17). This does not mean they are *responsible* for these souls, as though they were to answer in place of each person, but that they are entrusted with *governing* or *managing* them. The "account" that they will give is not for what *Christian's* did who were under their watch but for what *they* (the elders) did or did not do, and the way they did it. "Let them...with joy and not with grief"—i.e., do not make their job unnecessarily difficult by snubbing their concern, rejecting their counsel, or resisting their oversight. This is "unprofitable," since the elders will have to resort to discipline rather than edification. Also, the one causing such trouble will answer to Christ for his interference with the system which He has put into place. Those who were regularly forsaking the assembly of the saints (recall 10:25) are probably among those in need of this admonition.

"Pray for us" (13:18-19)—this indicates that the writer has not lost his confidence in those to whom he is writing, since he would not ask unbelievers to pray for anyone. After providing so much instruction to others, he still recognizes his own need for help. "The writer is trying

---

214 "The obligations of the Church and of her officers, are mutually binding. If it is the duty of the Elders to teach, it is also manifestly the duty of the other members of the Church to receive their lawful instructions; and if it is the duty of the former to rule, it is equally the duty of the latter to submit to all their acts of discipline which are not in violation of the law of Christ" (Milligan, *Commentary*, 380-381).

215 Yet Paul does warn that such men ought not to be questioned without sufficient evidence or witnesses. Bringing charges of sin against an elder is not impossible to do, but it is a most serious matter, given his leadership over the group and the effect such accusations will have *upon* that group (1 Tim. 5:19-21). I have much more to say on this subject in my *1 & 2 Timothy Commentary* and *Titus and James Commentary*; go to www.spiritbuilding.com/chad.

to say to the readers that he is aware of their uneasiness about his instruction and exhortations, but he himself bears no ill will."[216]

"Us" probably means himself and his fellow servants or ministers. But what is his personal situation? To what is he being "restored"—as a missionary, a minister, or elder? Has he been suffering with poor health? Is he in prison at the time of this writing, or simply in circumstances that prevent him from traveling freely (like Paul; see Rom. 1:13, 15:22-25)? We cannot know these answers for certain. We do know this: the writer takes his spiritual responsibilities very seriously, and thus puts high emphasis on his own moral conduct. He is not approved by "good conscience" alone; rather, he believes his conscience is "good" only because he has been approved by God because of his faith (recall 11:2).

Benediction and Final Thoughts (13:20-25)

It is apparent that the writer of *Hebrews* ends this letter in a far more personal way than he began it. The opening several chapters were instructional, educational, and theological. His epistle ends, however, with personal exhortations, fatherly appeals, and even requests for prayers for himself and his fellow workers. This proves that his motive was never merely to chastise them for their lack of focus as though he did not care about them personally. Instead, he shows his care for them throughout this epistle, but does so far more intimately in his final words than in his opening lessons.

The epistle is concluded with a magnificent doxology (hymn of praise), one that is filled with excellent truths (13:20-21). Having just spoken about the responsibility of church shepherds (elders), the writer now speaks of the "great Shepherd" who not only watches *over* our souls but *sanctifies* them (1 Peter 2:25, 5:4; see Isa. 40:11 and Ezek. 34:23). This Shepherd has no equal; His power, as displayed in His resurrection, is unprecedented and unparalleled; His blood does what no other blood can do.

---

216 Kistemaker, *NTC*, 428.

The "eternal covenant" refers to the salvation God has always provided for those who have called upon Him in faith, from one end of humanity to the other. While God has made several specific covenants with men over time, these are all summed up in one over-arching covenant: that of salvation by grace through faith in Christ (Rom. 1:17, Eph. 2:8). In this covenant, which fulfills all previous covenants, is the provision for absolute forgiveness of sins *and* everlasting fellowship with God *through* Christ's perfect atonement. It is eternal in its *purpose, scope* (or application), and *duration* (or perpetuity). This covenant of grace has always been predicated upon faith but required the blood of Christ to make it *real* and *viable*. This eternal covenant defines the "eternal purpose" in which we have "confident access" to God through "faith in Him" (Eph. 3:11-12).

With access to such power, wisdom, and grace, the faithful believer will never be unequipped, unprepared, or incapacitated. We are instructed to "do good" (recall 13:16) but it is Christ who empowers us to accomplish all good deeds in His name (Phil. 4:13). "Equip" here means to make complete or perfect, or to restore to an ideal state (as in Phil. 1:6, 2:13, and 1 Peter 5:10). God performs in *us* so that we can perform for *Him*. Indeed, we have been created anew in Christ for the purpose of performing good deeds (Eph. 2:10). All this is done "through Jesus Christ": we are never to forget that Christ is our righteousness, sanctification, and redemption (1 Cor. 1:30-31). He is Lord, we are servants; He is the head of His church, we are mere members of it; He is the Shepherd and Guardian of our souls, and He needs no advice or counsel from us. As He Himself said, "Apart from Me, you can do nothing" (John 15:5) with respect to salvation.

The "word of exhortation" (13:22) indicates an appeal to God's word as a means of instruction and edification (as Paul offered in Acts 13:15). If *Hebrews* is a "brief" letter, we can only imagine what the writer would have covered if given more opportunity. "Timothy" may likely be Paul's protégé to whom he wrote what we call *1 & 2 Timothy*. Given the means in which Paul used him, Timothy was probably well-known throughout the brotherhood at this point (13:23). Regardless, it appears that Timothy may have been in prison and had recently been released. There is no record of this in Paul's letters, since this imprisonment likely occurred after Paul's death (and the *Hebrews* letter was also likely written after his death).

"Leaders" here (as in 13:17) most naturally refers to elders. If the reference is to many elders, it would underscore the likelihood that this letter was sent to a circle of (Christian) *friends* and not to a single congregation (compare with, say, Phil. 1:1). "Saints" comes from a Greek word [*hagios*] which literally means "holy ones."[217] Saints are those who have been sanctified by Christ's blood and thus have been added to Christ's body (Rom. 1:7, 1 Cor. 2, etc.).

The expression "those from Italy" is difficult to interpret with certainty. Does he mean *he* is in Italy, or that he is sending greetings from *friends* who are in Italy? If he himself is in Italy, is he just passing through, or is that where he lives? Thankfully, this matter does not have to be resolved for us to accept the genuineness of this epistle. "Grace be with you all"—a common benediction, implying *we will overcome only with God's divine help.* Divine grace does everything for us that we cannot do for ourselves in the context of salvation.

---

217 Strong, *Dictionary* (electronic), G40.

Sources Used for Hebrews

Barnes, Albert. *Barnes' Notes,* vol XIII. Grand Rapids: Baker Book House, no date; orig. published by Blackie & Son (London), 1885.

Bruce, F. F. *The New International Commentary on the New Testament: Commentary on the Epistle to the Hebrews.* Grand Rapids: Wm. B. Eerdmans Publishing Co., 1964.

Clarke, Adam. *Clarke's Commentary* (vol VI). New York: Abingdon-Cokebury Press, no date; orig. published 1832.

Coffman, James Burton. *Commentary on Hebrews.* Austin, TX: Firm Foundation, 1971.

Hailey, Homer. *God's Eternal Purpose and the Covenants.* Louisville, KY: Religious Supply, 1998.

Jamieson, Robert, Andrew Fausset, and David Brown. *Commentary Critical and Explanatory on the Whole Bible (1871),* electronic edition. Database © 2012 by WORDsearch Corp.

Kistemaker, Simon J. *The New Testament Commentary: Exposition of Thessalonians, the Pastorals and Hebrews.* Grand Rapids: Baker Books, 1996.

Lenski, R. C. H. *Commentary on the New Testament: The Interpretation of the Epistle to the Hebrews and of the Epistle of James.* Grand Rapids: Hendrickson Publishers, 1998.

Lightfoot, Neil R. *Jesus Christ Today: A Commentary on the Book of Hebrews.* Abilene, TX: Bible Guides, 1976.

Lusk, David. *The God of the Covenant.* Mesa, AZ: self-published, 2002.

McClister, David. *A Commentary on Hebrews.* Temple Terrace, FL: Florida College Press, 2010.

Milligan, Robert. *The New Testament Commentary* (vol. IX). Delight, AR: Gospel Light, no date; orig. published 1868.

Robertson, Archibald Thomas. *Word Pictures in the New Testament* (vol. V). Grand Rapids: Baker Book House, 1960.

Strong, James. *Strong's Talking Greek-Hebrew Dictionary,* electronic edition. Database © 2003 by WORDsearch Corp.

Vines, W. E. *Vine's Expository Dictionary of New Testament Words.* STBC, no date; orig. published 1940.

Wuest, Kenneth S. *Word Studies in the Greek New Testament,* vol. II. Grand Rapids: Eerdmans Publishing Company, 1947; reprinted 1992.

www.ingramcontent.com/pod-product-compliance
Lightning Source LLC
Chambersburg PA
CBHW040304170426
43194CB00021B/2886